I0104869

Golden Years, Golden Hours

Stories and Reflections on Fly-fishing, Hunting and Aging

By Paul F. Vang

Dedication

For Kay, my beloved.

In the Broadway show, "Camelot," King Arthur sang, overly optimistically as it turned out, about "happy ever-aftering."

It's still a work in progress, but after 58 years together we have pretty much done it! You are my love and my rock.

Acknowledgements

Many of the stories in this book had their beginning in newspaper columns in the *Butte Weekly* of Butte, Montana, so I'm appreciative for the support of publishers and editors I've worked with, including the late Norlene Holt and Rick Foote, and, happily, still living, Robin Jordan and Linda Anderson.

I also appreciate support and encouragement from people who read my first book, *Sweeter than Candy*, and encouraged me to write another book.

A special thanks to Jerry, Alan, and Charley, friends and colleagues who reviewed my manuscript and offered feedback and positive reinforcement. As he did previously for *Sweeter than Candy*, Nick Gevock edited this book and made it better.

Our son, Kevin, the family's artistic mathematician, created the illustrations that are scattered through the chapters.

Copyright © 2020 by Paul F. Vang

Cover photo by Paul F. Vang
Illustrations by Kevin Vang

All rights reserved. No part of this book, either in part or in whole,
may be reproduced, transmitted or utilized in any form or by any means,
electronic, photographic or mechanical, including photocopying, recording,
or by any information storage and retrieval system, without permission in
writing from the publisher, except for brief quotations embodied
in literary articles and reviews.

Requests for permission to make copies of any part
of this book should be made to Five Valleys Press.

Quantity discounts are available *to your company or nonprofit*
for reselling, educational purposes, subscription incentives, gifts and
fundraising campaigns. For more information, please contact the publisher.

Five Valleys Press
6240 Saint Thomas Dr.
Missoula, Montana 59803

International Standard Book Number: 978-1-7353012-0-4

Table of Contents

Introduction   ix

Casting Through the Seasons
1	Muddling through Winter	1
2	Harbingers of Spring	5
3	Rites of Spring	11
4	April Showers	19

A Whiff of Summer
5	Something in the Air	27
6	Home Waters	33
7	Salmonflies: A tragic story of passion and violence on the Big Hole River	41
8	Salmonflies in the "Good Old Days"	45
9	Practicing for Patagonia	49
10	Dangerous Wildlife	53
11	A Baker's Dozen	57
12	A Love for Soft-Hackles	61
13	Murder on the Madison	65
14	Winning the One Fly Contest	69
15	A Modern Parable	73
16	Milo Goes Fishing	77

Excursions
17	The Trouble with Travel	85
18	Be Prepared	89
19	Duck Soup	93
20	Hexed in Michigan	97
21	Fishing with Optimism	105
22	New River	109
23	Grad School on Silver Creek	113
24	Prince of Wales	117
25	A Whopper of a Story	123
26	Fall Chinook	127

Critters

27	Don't Forget to Roll Up Your Windows	133
28	Bites	139
29	Urban Delicacies	145

A Change of Seasons

30	A Hint of Autumn	153
31	Shotgun Shopping	159
32	Grouse Training Camp	167
33	Passing the Torch	173
34	Milo Goes Hunting	177
35	Autumn Mixed Bag	181
36	Pheasant U	185
37	Perfection Happens	191
38	Life Goes On	203
39	The River in November	207
40	Tail Feathers	211
41	Orion the Hunter	215
42	Winter Can be Cruel	219
43	A Miracle Hunt	223
44	End of a Season	229
45	A Day Out of Kilter	237

Fishing and Hunting Through My Old Age Crisis

46	Old Age Crisis	241
47	On Being a Senior Citizen	247
48	Get an Early Start*	251
49	What the Hell, It's Just Money	255
50	A Happy Beginning to Life	263
51	A New Season	269

Introduction

On January 6, 2014, I first began putting down words for a new book.

That date has always had special meaning in our family.

Of course, on the Christian calendar, January 6 is Epiphany, celebrating the visit of the three wise men to the infant Jesus. It's also my dad's birthday, and if he were still living he'd now be 120 years old. Not surprisingly, he's been gone for many years, now, though he did live to within a few months of his 88th birthday.

He experienced many changes in his long life, from his boyhood home on a small farm in Norway, immigrating to the United States, and like millions of other immigrants, passed through Ellis Island on April 30, 1917. He was 17, and he worked at whatever jobs he could find, always with the goal of fulfilling his dream of owning his own farm.

He worked hard and even if he didn't get rich, he realized his dreams of farm ownership, and over the years earned recognition for sound conservation practices, in addition to a reputation for hard work.

While we remember him as a hard worker, we also recall his love of fishing. The work of the farm always came first, but if a rainy night made it impossible to put up hay or harvest crops, my brother, Carl, and I might look forward to his saying, "It's too wet to go in the fields. Why don't you go dig some worms and we'll go fishing."

He never had to ask us twice.

Fishing (and that meant angling for whatever might bite, including carp, suckers, bullheads, etc.) was my introduction to the outdoors. Fly-fishing Montana trout streams was still unforeseeable years into the future.

When I was around 10 or 11, a .22 rifle was under the Christmas tree, and a few years later my mother took me to a local hardware store to buy my first shotgun, a single shot 12-gauge gun.

I've accumulated a few, maybe quite a few, more fishing rods and guns over the years and I'm still enthusiastically using them, even if I sometimes wonder how many more years I'll still be able to say that. I'm in good health and live an active life. Still the years keep turning and I'm all too aware that the day is coming when I'll no longer be able to wade the trout streams or wander across the prairies and mountain foothills with a shotgun and Labrador retriever.

When that day comes it'll likely be a personal crisis of sorts. In the meantime I'll keep on casting and blasting through the seasons.

If I have some wisdom worth sharing about the aging process I'll try to include them in these pages, though I'll try to avoid getting too serious about it. It's not like I'm the first person to get old.

I'll note that, a few decades ago, I was too busy raising a family and working to have a mid-life crisis. Besides, the theme of fly-fishing through the mid-life crisis was taken.

Casting Through the Seasons

Chapter 1

Muddling Through Winter

"Come grow old with me. The best is yet to come." –Robert Frost

I often feel at loose ends this time of year. It's the in-between season when hunting seasons are over and it's still early for fly-fishing.

Not that there aren't things to do. It's the season for sorting through fly boxes and tying new creations to replace those lost in various willow trees, rocks, or, rarely, broken off by lunker trout. It's also ski season. Whether cross-country or downhill, skiing is a way to enjoy winter—not just endure it. Spending the winter months in some desert RV park doesn't appeal to me—not when I could be home enjoying winter on a ski slope.

Another way to pass time through the in-between season is to tie flies. I figure the fly-tying season begins after the Super Bowl—which means the season has begun.

I'll probably start by tying some midge patterns. I'm not usually a fan of midges but trout feed on midges in the winter months, so it's a good idea to give them what they want.

Some big and uglies come next. I know that some anglers use nothing but weighted Wooly Buggers, though frankly I don't get a lot of pleasure from chuck-and-duck fly-casting. Still, there are times when big and ugly flies are the only things that produce action, so I always make sure I have some on hand.

Next I'll do some of the fun stuff: small dry flies and nymphs, along with some soft-hackled wet flies. I think they're fun to tie and, even better, fun to use. I saved a couple patches of hide from a November white-tailed deer, so I'll make sure to tie some Humpies and deer-hair Caddis flies.

What I should do—and I tell myself this every summer when I'm trying to find a specific fly in one of my jumbled-together fly boxes— is simply throw out the whole mess and start over. Occasionally I peek into other people's fly boxes and I get this feeling of inferiority when I see their boxes full of perfectly tied flies, arranged in perfect rows.

I could throw everything out and start over, though I must admit that I still wouldn't have those rows of identical, perfectly tied flies. My flytying skills just aren't up to those standards, especially when it comes to cranking out perfect flies, dozens at a time. When I occasionally consider professional flytyers who sit down at their vise to turn out a couple gross of a particular pattern, I can't help but think it would be a perfect recipe for insanity.

Years ago, our son Kevin was a penniless graduate student at

Utah State University in Logan, Utah. To make some money he made a deal with a local fly-shop to tie a gross or two of pheasant tail nymphs. By the time he finished the project he was disabused of any notion that commercial fly-tying was going to be easy money. Though the flyshop was pleased with his product and would have taken more, he knew there had to be easier ways to pick up a few bucks.

If tying flies and dreaming about spring fishing aren't enough to get me past the post-hunting season blues, I'd better get busy and give my guns a good cleaning. After months of pounding brush and crossing barbed-wire fences, it's time to give those firearms a good scrubbing, inside and out, and touch-up any nicks in the stocks. Those healed-up scars on a gunstock give a gun character. An untreated gash tells more about the character of the person carrying the gun.

Finally, before I can say I've made a successful transition to the next season, I need to take time to go fishing—and I don't mean ice fishing, either. I don't catch many fish in winter, though I can't forget that my best fish of a recent year, a hook-jawed 20-inch brown trout, took a little nymph the first weekend of February. It wasn't a thrilling fight; fish are still pretty sluggish in the icy waters of winter.

Having a good fish on the end of my line not only cured the winter blues, it even enabled me to forget, for a few minutes, that my feet were frozen from hours of standing in the Madison River.

Of course, something I tend to do, while tying flies or standing in an icy river, is to let my mind wander, imagining and anticipating, whether the strike from a good fish, or recalling a highlight of the past hunting season.

Perhaps that's what keeps this old hunter and angler going from one season to the next: the anticipation that the next hunt or fishing outing will be the best ever.

It's all about memories: those of days past and those yet to be made.

Golden Years, Golden Hours

Chapter 2

Harbingers of Spring

"Woof, woof, woof, woof!"

It can be a challenge to figure out just what message your dog is sending. Does she have to go out? Does she want to come back in? She wants to check out the UPS guy? Maybe she just likes to hear her own voice.

This time I think I knew what she was talking about. I was standing in the icy waters of the Big Hole River for the first fishing outing of the season. A year earlier, by this time, I had been fishing half a dozen times, but that year we didn't have much snow and, consequently, the skiing was lousy. This year the skiing has been excellent and I'd been spending much of my outdoors time on the slopes.

I couldn't put it off any longer, though. My fishing urges were taking over. I hadn't tied as many flies as I'd intended but, rest assured, I have enough, so we were off to the Big Hole.

By "we," I include my black Lab, Flicka. At the time of this outing, Flicka was just about eight months old, and it was time to learn about fly-fishing. She'd had a half dozen hunting outings during the late fall and early winter. This fishing was new.

She ran along happily as I walked up the river to a favorite pool. Then things started to get strange. I stepped into the water and started wading out. Naturally Flicka followed. Then she started barking. I think I figured out the message her barking carried. From the way her teeth were chattering I think she was trying to tell me that the water was really cold and we should find some other entertainment. The air temperature was a relatively balmy 55 degrees—a nice day for March, but perhaps not if you're in a river and not wearing waders.

I tried to ignore her and get on with fishing. I might have been just as well off if I'd gone back on shore with her. The water was still too cold for the fish to be active. Aside from a few midges flitting about there wasn't any visible insect life.

Still, I knew the fish hadn't gone south for the winter. I felt a tug at the end of my line. I was just getting ready to tighten the line and catch the fish when Flicka jumped up on my legs. By the time I got her down and suitably admonished for jumping, the fish had slipped the hook. I could see it was a brown trout by its buttery-yellow belly when it jumped after getting off the hook.

That turned out to be the only fish action of the day and shortly after that I was happy to wade back out of the river and walk back to the access site and have some lunch while my feet warmed up. Lunch is something Flicka does understand, by the way.

That evening, black clouds gathered in the western skies and rain and snow began falling.

At home we received just a scant inch or so of snow, but our local ski area reported three inches of new snow, so a day later my neighbor and I went skiing. The powder of the day before had been groomed into the snowpack and skiing conditions were good. Warm sunshine softened the snow as the day progressed and on our last run of the afternoon the snow was just this side of slushy.

When I got home I schlepped the skis down to the basement and hung them up—this time for the season. The next day I ran the truck through the car wash to get rid of the mud that had accumulated on the last couple ski trips.

"To everything there is a season, a time for every purpose under the sun. A time to be born and a time to die, a time to plant and a time to pluck up that which is planted…"

Even if there's nothing mentioned in Ecclesiastes about either skiing or fishing, winter's over. It's time to fish.

A pheasant strutted along the top of the old railroad bed, his spring plumage shimmering a bright reddish-orange in the morning sunshine, contrasting with the freshly fallen snow. After several days of warm, sunny weather, Mother Nature reminded us once again that spring doesn't come on our schedule.

The mountains were a winter wonderland after the spring snowstorm, though the highway surface was warm enough so there was just a little slush on the road to the Madison River. Flicka and I were on our way in search of a feeding frenzy.

One of the harbingers of spring, as far as fly anglers are concerned, is the *baetis* mayfly, or blue-wing olive, depending on whether you prefer your bugs to speak Latin. This little mayfly emerges to become a flying insect in springtime, and again in the fall. For reasons best known to the mayflies, cool, damp weather is this mayfly's favorite time to become an adult.

People who like to fish the *baetis* hatch look for cool, damp, even snowy days to go fishing and that's why I was on the road.

On this morning along the Madison there are no other anglers. They likely know better than to be out. There was half a foot of fresh, fluffy snow on the riverbanks. Walking down the bank I learned, once again, how snow accumulates on the bottom of felt-bottomed boots. It's not easy walking with six inches of wet snow packed on the bottom of a boot. It was a chilly 25 degrees, though there was no wind— unusual for anywhere along the Madison River.

Before wading into the river I searched the surface for signs of mayflies floating along the surface, or for rises from trout picking off a bite of breakfast. Hopefully, I tied on a small dry fly, even though I couldn't spot any rises.

After getting no rises, I switched to a small soft-hackled nymph, which also drew no attention.

As I moved along the side of the river I saw a splashy rise along a seam where the water squeezed through an opening between a couple rocks, funneling bits of food toward a waiting trout. I quickly tied on another dry fly. It took several casts, but finally the fish decided the fly looked like food. It was just a 10-inch rainbow trout, but big enough to put a bend in my fly rod before I landed it and released it to go back and grow some more.

Feeding frenzy? I saw another rise a little further upstream, but nothing that came up to look at my fly, and, in fact, never had another bite the rest of the day.

We fly-fishers often head to streams and lakes in search of a feeding frenzy of one sort or another. It's part of that annual spring madness. On damp, chilly mornings we hope there will be a *baetis* hatch that turns on the trout. A few weeks later, depending on weather, we'll hope for that annual blizzard of bugs, the Mother's Day Caddis hatch. In June, anglers from all over the country will come to western Montana to get in on the salmon fly hatch.

Trying to coincide a day that's free for fishing with an insect hatch that turns big trout into a bunch of drunken frat boys is the dream that keeps us going through the winter. It's a guessing game, of course. That Mother's Day Caddis hatch does, indeed, get the fish going when conditions are right. On the other hand, it's more than likely that streams will be running high. While the bugs will do their thing regardless of what the river is doing, the fish may or may not notice, and may or may not bite on our humble imitations.

As for that day on the Madison, by noon the skies cleared and temperatures warmed, as the snow melted into the fresh, bright green grass. Still, the hatch happened. The snow along the river's edge was peppered with little mayflies that were drawn, for some reason, to the snow.

They missed the feeding frenzy, too.

Chapter 3

Rites of Spring

In spring a young man's fancy lightly turns to thoughts of love.
Alfred, Lord Tennyson.

Who am I kidding? At my…uh, middle age, my fancy turns to thoughts of fishing.

With the Vernal Equinox a few days ago, that day when the length of daylight and nighttime hours become approximately equal, the days will continue to lengthen until the summer solstice.

From the most ancient of times, spring has always been a time of new life and rebirth. I enjoy winter, but when spring comes I eagerly seek out signs of the season, whether it's tulips emerging in my flowerbeds to the return of robins. The rhythm of the seasons is the rhythm of life.

Last week I passed up the revelry of St. Patrick's Day in Butte to head for the Beartrap Canyon area on the lower Madison River.

I could bore you with stories of how I caught and released one fish after another, reaffirming my self-concept as a skilled and lucky fly fisherman. The truth, sad to say, is uglier. I got skunked. I also managed to get my line tangled several times, an inevitable complication to using two flies.

If we anglers have a reputation for occasionally stretching the truth, let's face reality. We lie because the truth is too ugly. As an example of the ugliness of truth, I had a streamside conversation with an angler who said he had all sorts of action, including catching a bunch of trout on dry flies. Assuming he wasn't lying, that meant I couldn't say, "The fish weren't biting." I just couldn't catch them.

In his book, *Pavlov's Trout*, Paul Quinnet, a behavioral psychologist, writes, "Many people think fishermen are born liars. This is not true. Fishermen acquire the talent. They start out lying to themselves and, before they know it, they're lying to anyone who'll listen." This confirms, from the scientific point of view, the wisdom of the late humorist Ed Zern, who wrote, "Fishermen are born honest, but they get over it."

Quinnett discusses steelhead fanatics in the Pacific Northwest, where he lives, who go to great lengths to stand in an icy river for hours, making thousands of casts and still not catch a fish. From the psychologist's standpoint, the fishermen could be classified as certifiably insane. Another professional assessment: he lies to himself.

The good fisherman, Quinnett says, is an eternal optimist. He actually believes that he's going to catch fish. In fact, he's going to catch a fish on the next cast. For the successful angler, "The glass is not half full. It's filling and about to run over."

Tom McGuane, the Montana-based novelist, screenwriter and essayist, touched on this topic in his book, *The Longest Silence*, a collection of fishing essays. He says he doesn't wish to compete with others. "I…do most of my fishing alone so that I may better absorb its mysteries, poetry, and intimations of mortality. The lone angler may fish and dawdle as he pleases. He may even catch fish." When rejoining the company of others, he can dispense with competition by lying about his results. "So, all is well. A day in the life has been suitably taken in, and in this avalanche of lies, a kind of truth has been served. The only people any the wiser are the general public."

But I digress.

I did have a couple hits on my flies, including one that danced at the end of my line for a few seconds before slipping the hook. I had the satisfaction of knowing there were two fish in the river with the good taste and common sense to take at least a slightly more than casual glance at my flies.

I also know there will be other days.

As blood slowly seeped from the cut on my finger, I idly wondered whether the blood dripping from my finger could be construed as chumming for fish—and whether chumming was legal. I concluded that as neither sharks nor piranhas live in the Big Hole River a few drops of blood wouldn't trigger any kind of feeding frenzy or draw a citation.

After months of not catching fish, things occasionally seem awkward and something as mundane as unhooking and releasing a fish becomes hazardous—to me at least. I'm not sure just how I did it, but as the brown trout slowly swam away, I realized that my finger hurt where I'd jabbed it with the fishhook. On the bright side, a puncture wound that bleeds is one not likely to become infected.

On an even brighter side, now that spring has officially happened, I've caught some fish.

On one of those first days of spring it was warm and sunny, so Flicka and I headed for a favorite stretch of water on the Big Hole. It wasn't exactly a feeding frenzy, but in a couple hours of fishing I caught three fish; two browns and a rainbow, plus hooked a couple other fish that were on for a moment before escaping the hook.

Here in the mountain west we take our seasons as they come, and spring is a season that comes by fits and starts. Since that so-called first day of spring we had the heaviest snowfalls of the entire winter season—snowfalls that did a lot to bring our snowpack up to the normal range in most of southwest Montana's river drainages.

On the second day of spring, some two and a half weeks later, Flicka and I went fishing again. This time we improved the head count, catching two brown trout and two rainbow trout. Interestingly, all four fish, as well as the three fish I caught on that earlier outing, all got hooked on the same fly—not just the same pattern; the same fly. I tried other flies, of course, but that's what caught them.

What is that hot fly? It was a San Juan Worm, a fly developed for fishing the San Juan River in New Mexico, though it certainly catches fish in lots of places, including the Big Hole River in early spring.

As spring progresses I'll be out more often, though the fishing can be changeable, depending on surges of runoff, insect activity and fish activity, as warming waters increase metabolism rates.

There are cautions, however. First, it's important to be careful when wading in these early outings. The water isn't much warmer than the ice was a few days earlier. A dunking this time of year could be a critical mistake. A related factor is that after a relatively short time of standing in the river, feet get cold and numb, and numb, half-frozen feet are clumsy feet, especially if you, like me, have pin-hole leaks in your waders. Just remember the title of one of John Gierach's books, *Death, Taxes, and Leaky Waders*. Leaky waders are just one of those inevitabilities—like beating that April 15 tax deadline.

It's also important to know regulations. Here in Montana, the third Saturday in May is the standard opening day of the fishing season. On some waters you can fish year around. Other waters are open for fishing but it's catch-and-release only, and still other waters are plumb closed until that Saturday in May. Occasionally, some people complain, "You have to have a lawyer along to interpret the regs." I don't think it's that complicated, though you do have to know where you are and what the rules are.

In spite of cold feet and other challenges, I like early season fishing. There are no crowds or squadrons of drift boats. The countryside is awakening. We've made it through the winter. It's worth celebrating.

*"When it's springtime in the Rockies, I am coming back to you...
Once again I'll say, 'I love you.' While the birds sing all the day
When it's springtime in the Rockies. In the Rockies, far away."*

Unless you set an alarm, you probably missed it.

Spring, or the Vernal Equinox, to be precise, happens, in most years, on March 20, and usually in the wee hours of the morning in the Mountain time zone. It marks the moment when the sun crosses the equator, and day and night is of nearly equal length everywhere in the world.

Of course, we who live in the Rocky Mountain West know that the astronomical beginning of spring doesn't mean much when it comes to actually having spring-like weather.

In western Montana spring weather often means mild, sunny days, and cold, snowy days. Temperatures ranging from below zero to the mid-50s often follow each other. In short, anything goes.

At our house, I start looking for tulips to be emerging around the first of March, along with green shoots from garlic I planted last fall. Robins start showing up in mid-March. Also, in mid-March, I often see chives emerging in the garden, the first edible garden green of the season. In coming weeks those chives will keep a standing appointment with a baked potato or tossed salad. Naturally, often as not, the day after those chives emerge they might be covered with a thick blanket of snow.

Unsettled, fickle weather is all too typical of this time of year, and, again, in September at the time of the autumnal equinox. There's something about the equal days and nights that seems to cause weather changes, and thus spring snowstorms come on the heel of April showers, and the in the fall, hot, dry weather will often be interrupted with cold rain and early snowfall.

"Springtime in the Rockies" also refers to one of the standards in the American Songbook. The lines of the chorus bring to mind images of bright sunshine and apple blossoms. Artists, diverse as Gene Autry, Leadbelly, the Sons of the Pioneers, and Frankie Yankovic, have recorded the song.

"Springtime in the Rockies" is also the title for two old movies. The first, made in 1937, starred Gene Autry. It likely had a different storyline than the 1942 musical comedy remembered as the starring debut of the 1940s pinup girl, Betty Grable.

I enjoy winter but for now, fly-fishing is taking priority in the scheme of things. It's time to take those bits of steel, hair and feathers and dunk them in a Montana river to see if those hot new patterns written up in the glossy magazines actually produce fish.

It's time to hang snow shovels in the garage and start looking at garden seeds. The time for serious gardening in our mountain climate doesn't start for another two months, yet the urge to scratch in the dirt and scatter seeds is getting stronger.

At the same time, I look at weather forecasts and wonder if there might be some fresh snow before our local ski area closes for the season.

Chapter 4

April Showers

"Though April showers may come your way/they bring the flowers that bloom in May..."

The voice of Al Jolson crooned from the radio. Dave tried to lift his head from the table but it hurt too much. If he had the strength he would have thrown a bottle at the radio to stop the incessant noise breaking into his well-earned hangover.

"Millie!" He raised his voice to get his wife's attention and immediately realized his mistake. In a barely audible whisper, he continued, "Millie, please. Could you turn that radio down?"

Millie walked over to the radio and Al Jolson became more tolerable.

Dave's pounding head began to relax a little, and he no longer pictured Jolson in blackface, wailing away on one song after another.

Millie bustled around the kitchen. She turned on a burner and tossed slices of bacon into a well-blackened cast iron fry pan. "Dave," she said, "we've been married over 30 years, and we've been through a lot. But I just don't understand you anymore." She started mixing pancake batter, and then put the pottery bowl back down on the counter with a crack that Dave felt way down in the middle of his head.

"Millie, do you mind?"

"I mind, alright. I mind that every night you drink yourself into a stupor, and then you spend every day recovering from another hangover." Millie turned the bacon and turned back to Dave. "You're killing yourself, and you're killing me and you're killing our marriage. We can't go on like this any longer."

Dave got himself off the kitchen chair and limped to the kitchen sink and ran some cold water in his hands, splashing some in his face, as well as over the countertop and floor. He groped through the air until he felt a towel. He turned and said, "Mil,' I'm sorry. I know it's wrong. But I think of the boys and imagine they're coming home." He sat back down and gripped the coffee mug and, bitterly, continued. "And they're never coming back. When I'm drinking seems like the only time I can get those telegrams out of my sight."

The war had been over for almost four years now, and the names of distant battlegrounds were fading from the memory of most people. For Dave and Millie, however, not a day went by without pain. The banner in the front window, with its two gold stars, was fading, but in Dave's eyes, the red borders in the banner dripped with blood, and thoughts of those distant battlefields in North Africa and the Pacific haunted him.

The couple ate quietly. Millie understood how much Dave had suffered. It's not any easier for me, she thought, but she kept busy living each day as it came, knowing that all the whiskey in Kentucky wouldn't bring their sons home.

"Dave." Millie intruded into his thoughts. "Dave, why don't you go fishing? The ice went off the river a couple weeks ago, and after the rain last night, the fish should be biting. I'd like some trout for dinner."

It had been a long tine since Dave had gone fishing. When the boys were growing up, they went fly-fishing just about every weekend. After the war, though, the thought of fishing seemed to profane the memories of his sons.

"Dave, do it!" Millie had had enough of Dave's self pity. She packed a lunch and then helped him round up his old hip boots and vest. Then she picked a metal rod tube from the corner of the closet. She shoved him out the door and helped him load things in the old Plymouth. Dave started to say, "B...b...but, Mil..."

"But nothing. Go fishing and bring me some trout."

It was a lonely drive to the river, but Dave made it and parked at what had been one of their favorite spots. It had been a long time, but the old routine of soaking leaders and putting on waders seemed familiar. He pulled the rod tube out of the trunk and suddenly stopped. This was the brand new Montague fly rod the boys had given him just before they shipped out. "First thing we do when we get home, Dad," Billy said, "is we're going fishing."

Dave pulled the cloth bag and the sections of bamboo rod out of the tube and was startled to see a piece of paper fall to the ground. Trembling, he picked it up and, with a shudder, recognized the writing. The words read:

Dad, if you're reading this note, it probably means we're not coming home, because we figured you wouldn't use this rod until we got back. We agreed that whoever got home first would remove this note. Dad, we had wonderful times growing up, fishing, hunting, and roaming the countryside. We're anxious to come home but if it is not to be, just remember that we love you and Mom and we have no regrets. Go fishing and catch a few for us.

Tears welled as he assembled the rod and walked to the river. He tied on a fly and began casting. It seemed unreal, somehow, but after an hour of fishing, he had two nice trout in the creel.

Walking back to the car, he looked for fresh ferns in which to wrap the fish for the trip home. Next to a slushy snow bank, crocuses bloomed in the spring sunshine.

Driving home, it seemed Dave saw things with an unfamiliar clarity. He saw bald eagles perching on trees above the river, and Canada geese flying over the water. Hereford calves frolicked in greening pastures, and he could hear the call of meadowlarks above the whisper of the warm spring air.

Millie heard the car drive in the yard. She expected to hear the sound of breaking glass, as she had so often these last few years. Instead, she saw Dave walk to the house with a bounce in his stride, holding the lid of the creel open for her to see the fish. "Start cookin,' Hon."

They got in the house and after putting his fishing equipment away he began studying the calendar on the kitchen wall. "Hey, Mil,'" he asked, "What day is this?"

"It's Saturday. You know that."

"Yeah, I know, but which Saturday?"

Millie walked over and planted her finger on a square and said, "It's this Saturday. Tomorrow's Easter."

Dave then surprised her more than she believed possible. "Can we go to church tomorrow?

Millie stood there a moment, not believing her ears. "Yes. Yes, we'll go to church."

They stood for a moment, looking at each other, and then flew into each other's arms and, locked in embrace, they sobbed uncontrollably, as the dam of tears finally broke free.

"Millie," Dave finally said, "we're going to make it."

Golden Years, Golden Hours

A Whiff of Summer

Golden Years, Golden Hours

Chapter 5

Something in the Air

The warmer weather of late spring and early summer instigated activity in our neighborhood, as people emerged from winter hibernation to take down storm windows, rake yards and maybe scatter a few seeds in gardens. No doubt we'll have more frosty mornings and even snow, but we enjoy mild, summer-like weather when we can get it.

It's also refreshing, after months of having the house closed up, to go to bed at night with the windows open to cooling breezes.

On a couple nights, however, the evening breezes brought something more than that earthy smell of spring. There was no ignoring it, either. There is nothing quite so unmistakable than a whiff of skunk scent in the air.

I recall a long ago *National Geographic* article about the powerful ability of scents to trigger memories. A light whiff of cloves, for example, reminds me of carnations, which in turn reminds me of high school proms and awkward moments when my date and I exchanged flowers.

The distinctive scent of skunk in the air triggers other memories.

Skunks have a pair of scent glands at the base of their tail and are able to accurately send streams of a thick, oily liquid at any person or other animal, especially dogs, that they feel are threatening them. Alas, skunks frequently carry rabies, so a confrontation with a skunk is not only unpleasant but also dangerous.

The basic diet of skunks is insects and grubs and in the wild they will diligently search meadows and wetlands for food, often coming across pheasant or duck nests, and will gladly eat their fill in eggs, thus becoming significant predators of game birds.

Skunks seem well adapted to urban life, finding suitable habitat in neglected corners, ditches, hedges and creek bottoms. They are mostly nocturnal, so we seldom see them in the daytime, but on warm spring and summer evenings they occasionally remind us of their presence.

I've been lucky and neither our dogs nor I have ever had a nasty encounter with our striped friend, though we've had some close calls.

Years ago, while visiting our in-laws in Glendive, Montana, a skunk wandered through the neighborhood and the evening air was heavy with skunk aerosol. I don't know just how close it was but Sam, our Labrador retriever of the time, caught a light dose. We scrubbed her down that night, but all the same I'm glad it was our children that shared the back seat with Sam for the ride home the next day.

A couple times our Labs have come uncomfortably close to skunks while out in the field. Luckily I was able to persuade them—perhaps terrify would be more accurate—to back off and avoid trouble.

Another memory triggered by the skunk-scented evening air was from my childhood, when my uncle Syvert and his wife, Jenny, came from Norway to spend the summer with us on our southern Minnesota farm. By August he was terribly homesick and wanted nothing more to do with anything American. He learned the distinctive odor of skunk one evening. A few nights later, we had some of the first sweet corn of the season and he remarked that, "The skunk smelled better than the corn."

I don't know where we went wrong. After growing up in small towns in rural areas of Montana and the Midwest, our daughter, Erin, turned into a sushi-eating urbanite.

She lives in the hills of Oakland, California. The hills are a long way, in several ways, from the congested, sometimes blighted areas near the city center and waterfront. It's an area of steep, forested canyons, with fancy homes and distant views of San Francisco Bay.

There's also a surprising amount of wildlife in these hills. At any time you might see wild turkeys or blacktail deer feeding on a hillside. Bobcats and raccoons also roam the hills.

In early spring, one year, she began to notice an odor around the house. It wasn't there all the time, though enough to be annoying. She was in the middle of work projects, and with the rainy season in progress, she didn't have the time or inclination to slog up a muddy hillside to check things out on one of those dark and rainy nights. Meanwhile the smell grew worse.

She looked out the windows, went out on the decks of her house and peered up the hillside. She checked the crawlspace under the house. Finally, the weather broke and she put on her hiking boots and went hunting. She found the source. Under a deck in back of her house, she found a dead deer. She didn't know how, when or why it died.

All we really know is that, in what might be the ultimate fantasy for many Bay Area dwellers, the deer finally found off-street parking and died and went to heaven.

Mother Nature is relentlessly efficient. Nothing ever goes to waste, and sooner or later all living things return to the soil. Unless you're a bear sniffing the air after a long hibernation, however, it isn't necessarily pleasant.

Spring fishing is a case in point. I occasionally find dead animals along or in rivers in springtime. Deer, moose, cows and beavers are examples of river bottom casualties I've come across. A fatal slip or fall through the ice is usually the cause of most of these animal deaths. Somehow, most of these souvenirs of winter get carried away with spring runoff.

There's a small dam on the upper Missouri River, not far downstream from where the Madison, Gallatin and Jefferson Rivers join to form the Mighty Mo. Somehow, I can picture, in my mind, the backwaters above the dam full of dead critters bobbing around like driftwood. It's something to keep in mind when I get thirsty on a hot summer day and am tempted to scoop up a drink of river water.

Dead critters don't have to be large to raise a stink. I recall finding a dead mouse in the back of our car's glove compartment that certainly made its presence known. I also remember when the family car was afflicted with a rank odor. I followed my nose and found the source. A can of angleworms had been left in the trunk after a mid-summer fishing outing a couple weeks earlier.

Erin also tells of a friend who loaned her car to friends who took a road trip up the coast for fresh seafood for their Christmas party. By mid-January she noticed a terrible odor. She searched the car and in the trunk found one formerly living oyster that had fallen out of a cooler and died. She learned from that oyster's penalty for over-parking that, "Big smells can come from small packages."

Incidentally, in 2017 Erin decided she'd had enough of urban living and moved back (and I use the word "back" advisedly, as she hadn't actually lived in Montana since she finished second grade back in 1973) to Montana. She probably still eats sushi, but she'd now question my calling her an urbanite.

Golden Years, Golden Hours

Chapter 6

Home Waters

While figuring out whether it's spring, summer, or a revisit of winter is a daily game, there's no question that bountiful rains are great for our lawns, gardens and the countryside in general.

The New York Times, one June, carried an early June report from eastern Wyoming, an area that had abundant rainfall that spring. "Take it as a rule of Wyoming life: a wet rancher is a happy rancher. And right now, many of the ranchers in the state are sopping and grinning."

There is nothing like spring rain to turn the countryside green, especially if that's coupled with the knowledge that there's a good snowpack up in the mountains to back it up.

The first weekend of June, my wife and I got out for a camping weekend, and this time, for a change, we got it right. We had mild weather and lots of sunshine for a weekend on the upper Big Hole River.

The fishing? Let's not go there. Let's say it's a great time of the year for floaters, even if it's not particularly productive for this wade angler.

There's more to these camping weekends than fishing, thankfully. Mother Nature is hard at work putting on this year's flower show, and it's only going to get more spectacular as we move into full-fledged summer.

The weekend was also for the birds. In addition to the many swallows cruising along the river's surface for emerging insects, songbirds of all kinds were flitting about the riparian areas. On a couple evenings we could hear, from across the river, a ruffed grouse drumming, advertising his availability for female companionship.

It's one of those unique sounds of nature. The first time I heard it I thought it was somebody trying to start a stubborn lawnmower that fires up, runs well for a few seconds and then dies again. When I realized the sound was coming from a timbered hillside I knew it was a drumming ruffed grouse, not a lawnmower. The next evening my wife was able to hear the grouse, as well—her first time.

I fished a creek that feeds into the river and heard another drumming ruffed grouse in the dense willows. My Lab, Flicka, picked up the scent and decided I could fish if I like; she was going hunting. She flushed the bird and returned full of excitement.

Another bird made it clear whose territory we were visiting. Kay had gotten a package of chicken breasts out of the trailer's freezer for our dinner that evening and set it out on the picnic table to thaw in the warm sunshine.

I came back from fishing and noted that the package was half-empty and what was left looked like a bird had pecked at it. I left the package on the table and Kay, who until I came back hadn't noticed the depredation, got something else out of the freezer for dinner. In a few minutes the thief returned. It was a crow that made the happy discovery of free food and he/she came back for more. We watched and photographed as the crow pecked at the chicken, cutting chunks out and flying across the river with its treasure.

That was one happy crow. He came back one more time after the chicken was gone in search of more treats but this time left disappointed.

Sometimes there is such a thing as a free lunch, but it's not necessarily an all-you-can-eat buffet.

After an afternoon of fishing, I put my fly rod on the top of the car while I took off my waders and other fishing gear. When I got home, about an hour later, I started putting gear away and came to an empty rod tube. I apparently drove off with my rod still on top of the car. I told Kay what happened and said, "I'm going back to look for it."

It was almost dark when I got there. The rod wasn't anywhere in the area. I felt devastated. I'd built the rod myself a year earlier, so it was essentially a one of a kind. It was a long, sad trip home, and when I finally got there I sat down at the table for a dinner that had been warming in the oven far too long.

The phone rang. "Is this Paul Vang?" a man asked.

"Yes," I said.

"Were you fishing down by the Notch this afternoon?"

"Yes, I was."

"I've got your rod. I almost drove over it."

After building my rod I engraved my initials on the rod's butt cap. When my caller got home to Dillon, he went through the area phone book and looked in every community listing for someone who would have the initials, PFV. My name was the only one that seemed to fit, so he called.

As it worked out, his wife was coming to Butte the next morning to take her sister to the airport, so we arranged to meet.

The next day I not only had my rod back, I had yet another great reason to love the Big Hole… and my guardian angel from Dillon, Montana.

It most likely has something to do with atmospheric pressure changes that affect a trout's appetite. The winds on this Big Hole River canyon were swirling about. One moment the wind was blowing from downstream. A minute later, the winds did a 180 and were blowing from upstream. Temperatures were comfortable on the bank, but in mid-river the wind felt icy.

It was tough casting, especially with the ultra-light fly rod I love to use in mid-summer, but I saw a fish strike my dry fly and it went tearing down the river to shed that sudden interruption in its routine. A couple minutes later I landed the fish, a brightly marked rainbow trout. I slid the hook out of its jaw and watched it swim off, hopefully not much worse for wear.

As it turned out that was the only fish I caught that day. I suppose I shouldn't admit to such underwhelming results. As some writers suggest: never let the truth stand in the way of a good story.

That's okay. The point of this day of fishing wasn't as much to catch fish as it was stress management. On our refrigerator is one of those "Duckboy" postcards showing a photo of a couple guys standing in a river with fly rods, with the caption, "Stress-Management

Seminar in Montana." There's a lot of truth in that caption.

We all have stress in our lives, of course. I quickly noticed that when I retired from my former career as a government manager the stress level in my life went down considerably. Still, getting away from one source of stress doesn't spare us from others.

There's something about flyfishing; the process of standing in the middle of a river, with currents swirling all around, focusing your mind on picking out a fly that you hope imitates the right insect and directing your energies on casting into the wind and getting a good drift of the fly. Sometimes we're rewarded with a rising fish; sometimes we're not.

Perhaps it's also a good reminder that sometimes it isn't all about us. We can study, scheme, practice techniques, tie the most seductive flies, buy the finest fishing rods, and still it all boils down to whether a trout, with a brain the size of a pea, will let a sudden impulse get the better of its judgment and decide to eat this strange-looking bug that's floating across its cone of vision.

We might think that with our advanced education, years of fishing experiences, good fishing equipment, and all the trappings of modern flyfishing wisdom, a good angler could catch fish almost at will.

It doesn't work that way, though certainly some people are more successful than others. We sometimes talk about the 80/20 theory when it comes to fishing. That is, as a general rule, 80 percent of the fish are caught by 20 percent of the anglers, a theory with applications to other endeavors, as well.

A good question might be whether I'm among the successful 20 percent. A good question, but I'm afraid the answer might cause stress.

Mother's Day is observed the second Sunday in May. That much we know. Mother's Day came right on schedule, and we duly observed the protocols for the day.

What we're waiting for now is the Mother's Day Caddis Hatch, that explosion of insect life that seems to get the flyfishing season going in earnest.

There are many kinds of caddisflies, and trout depend on them for a big chunk of their diet. The late Gary LaFontaine, in his landmark book, *Caddisflies*, cited scientific studies that estimate that caddisflies account for 44.7 percent of aquatic foods eaten by trout, significantly more than mayflies and stoneflies, though mayfly and stonefly imitations usually take up more space in a fly shop's cases.

Caddisflies are of the scientific order of *Trichoptera*, and, according to LaFontaine, there are more than 1200 species in 142 genera and 18 families known in North America, and over 7,000 species known world-wide, and about now I'm wishing I remembered more from those high school biology classes.

The scientific name for the Mother's Day Caddis is *Brachycentrus*, and a common name for them is Grannom. The caddis hatch happens on most western rivers. The trick is being around when it happens, as well as having fishable water.

The Mother's Day Hatch, when it finally happens, can be impressive. The hatch on the Yellowstone River is famed for profuse hatches, when large rafts of insects float along the river's currents, and an angler trying to get in on the action may find caddisflies crawling all over his/her face and into ears. On the Big Hole River, where I do most of my fishing, I don't think I've ever seen any hatches that dense, though when there are clouds of insects buzzing around trees and bushes it's still impressive, especially when they crawl inside your glasses.

On the other hand, by the time these masses of bugs appear on the water's surface, as well as buzzing around trees and bushes, the trout may have already filled their bellies with emerging caddis trying to make their way from the stream's rocky bottom to the surface. In fact, a good strategy, during the hatch, can be to use an emerger-type fly such as the sparkle pupa patterns developed by LaFontaine, or a green-bodied soft-hackle fly.

As for fishable water, in most years that's the real trick. All too often, the Hatch happens when spring runoff is really getting going, and while there are lots of caddisflies buzzing around, the trout are hunkered down, and not spending a lot of time looking up at adult insects on the water's surface. I know I've had my best caddis action in years when runoff was more on the tame side.

There can be a fine line for optimal caddis hatch conditions. I fondly remember one spring on the Big Hole the water was running on the high side, though it wasn't blown out. Shoreline willows were partially submerged, and trout were hanging right in the willows, in position to pick off caddis bugs dropping on the water. I had a banner day, though the wading often seemed adventurous.

There are many caddisfly imitations available, whether you roll your own or buy them at a fly shop. Caddisfly imitations generally fall into several categories, depending on whether you're trying to imitate a cased larva on the bottom of the stream, the pupa swimming through the water column, or the adult winged insect.

As mentioned earlier, green-bodied soft-hackle wet flies or LaFontaine sparkle pupa are good pupa imitations. The Elk Hair Caddis, developed by the late Al Troth, is certainly one of the standards. I've also had success with a Renegade, a simple fly that possibly suggests a pair of mating caddis to a hungry trout. A small Humpy is also effective, especially when there are both caddisflies and mayflies buzzing around. If you don't mind tangled flies and tippets, this may also be a good time for a dry fly with a wet fly dropper.

Best of all, once caddisflies show up, fish will be looking at caddisflies until fall.

Golden Years, Golden Hours

Chapter 7

Salmonflies: A tragic story of passion and violence on the Big Hole River

It's salmonfly time, again. It's that time of year when southwest Montana's premier trout stream, the Big Hole River, becomes a mixture of a California freeway at rush hour, a healthy dose of carnival and a little bit of zoo thrown in for good measure.

It's that time of year when *Pteronarcys californica*, the giant stonefly of western rivers, crawls from the river's streambed towards shore where it creeps out of the water and shinnies up shoreline vegetation, such as tall grass or a willow branch, and becomes an adult. Yes, becoming an adult means exactly that, though there is that little detail of crawling out of its own exoskeleton first.

In that shining moment of the salmonfly's life, the ugly nymph becomes a lovely (at least to other stoneflies) adult, ready for a little adult action. That brief fling at the joys of adulthood results in one final flight to lay eggs on the river's surface.

Let us imagine, for the moment, a pair of salmonflies, we'll call them Ole and Lena, perched at the top of a willow branch, aglow with connubial bliss.

"Ah, that was mighty nice, Lena." Ole stretched out his body, all two inches of it, with pleasure, craving, inexplicably, a cigarette.

"I often wondered what this day might be like," Lena replied. "Crawling around on the bottom of the river was getting tedious. I knew there was more to life than hiding under rocks and eating bits of leaves."

"I know what you mean," Ole agreed. "It was also getting dangerous. It seemed every time I peeked out, there was a fish lurking around. That, and watching out for fishermen walking around and stomping on us."

"Uff da," Lena exclaimed, "would you believe I came from a family with five thousand brothers and sisters and I'm the only one who made it to a wedding day."

"You too? Ah, Lena, that is just too much of a coincidence. We're both orphans, and now we're the last of our family." Ole added. "I personally saw half a dozen of my brothers lose their footing yesterday, and they were gone."

"Yah, and getting out of the river was no picnic either. Crawling up that willow branch wasn't as easy as it looked, and then being stuck there all night as I crawled out of my exoskeleton. I was kind of wishing I were back in the water; it hurt so much. I was wishing I hadn't eaten that last bit of bark yesterday."

Ole shook off a sudden urge for potato chips, remembering that now that he was an adult he no longer had a digestive system. With that reality check, he returned his attentions to Lena. "Hey sweetie," he whispered, "you suppose we could…you know, try that again?"

Lena smiled seductively, "Ole, you rascal, you. Ah, what the heck, come here, big guy."

The afternoon sun dropped down below the tops of the cotton-wood trees. Lena shivered a bit in the cooling air. "Ole, my beloved, I just happened to think; were you using some kind of protection?"

Ole blinked. "Protection? What do you mean?"

"What do I mean?" Lena barked back. "You lousy so and so, you got me pregnant! Oh, Ole, I'm pregnant and now I have this irresistible urge to fly down to the river. I have 5,000 fertilized eggs to get rid of and it's all your fault!"

With that, Lena spread her wings. With her heavy load of eggs, she struggled to get airborne before finally setting a course for mid-river.

With a sense of foreboding, Ole called out, "Lena, be careful!"

Lena dipped her extended body into the water, expelling eggs, while her wings fluttered helplessly on the surface. She was just about to call back to Ole when a trout, attracted by the surface commotion, ate Lena with a single gulp.

Ole, devastated with shock and grief, watched the now silent river from his vantage point on the willow branch. Perhaps this overwhelming feeling of desperate loneliness is why he didn't see the golden flash of a western tanager swooping down on him.

His final thoughts, before that fatal crunch, were, "Lena! Lena! My love, my life."

Golden Years, Golden Hours

Chapter 8

Salmonflies in the "Good Old Days"

People occasionally tell me that we don't have salmonfly hatches on the Big Hole River like in the "good old days." My personal experience with these stonefly hatches goes back around 30 years, so they may be right.

The salmonfly hatch can be a bit elusive, as it's not something you can mark on the calendar. The old Butte tradition that it should be happening at Melrose on Miners Union Day, June 13, may be a fairly good hunch, though it's not something to rely on.

Still, with luck, it's possible to hit the hatch at its peak and, if so, you might get the idea that the good old days might not be way back when.

Several days before Miners Union Day, I went fishing on the Big

Hole River near Wise River. I was hoping the hatch might be on and it didn't take long to find out. Walking along the river's edge, I quickly noticed occasional salmonflies taking to the air, and when I took a closer look at the willows, I could see salmonflies almost everywhere, some by themselves and some that were coupled together, doing what couples often do.

Of course, another indication of the salmonfly hatch was the volume of boat traffic. There was a constant parade of drift boats and rubber rafts floating by, with anglers pounding the shallows with their versions of imitations of the real thing.

I'm not complaining, as I'm often among them in my pontoon boat. I am convinced, however, that the numbers of boaters and anglers do put the fish off their feed. In a couple hours, I had just a couple rises that didn't result in hookups.

After a lunch break I walked in a different direction, also noting an increase in salmonfly activity, including having many big bugs landing on me.

I found a little stretch of water that had been mostly left alone, as boats have to swing wide to avoid getting sucked into an irrigation diversion. I had just tied on a fresh fly and tossed it out in the water, while pulling line off my reel for a cast. Then, "bang!" a good-sized rainbow trout hit my fly. I landed and released the fish and on my next cast I again had a strike and this fish was hot! It raced across the current and around a rock bar on the other side of the diversion. It finally stopped and I was luckily able to pull the fish over the bar, and eventually landed it. It was another good rainbow, with some cutthroat markings on its lower jaw.

I had another momentary hookup, and a couple more rises. A brief rain shower came through and insect activity paused. After the shower moved on, the sun came out and there was a sudden explosion in stonefly activity. They were everywhere, and at one point I had three or four bugs on my shirt, another on the bill of my cap, and a couple more on my neck.

46

Adult stoneflies don't bite or sting, so they're harmless. Still, it reminded me of my old friend, the late Bill Pesanti, who told of driving upriver for a family picnic. He found a picnic spot on the river and before he got the food out, his kids ran, screaming, back to the car, because the big stoneflies were swarming around them.

Still, we'll be thankful to our Creator that He didn't make mosquitoes this big!

While stoneflies of one kind or another reach the adult stage of life through much of the year, there is certainly a peak of activity in June. Besides the big salmonflies, I also saw big golden stones, small golden stones, and other, smaller, stoneflies.

The peak of the salmonfly hatch also marked the peak of runoff on the Big Hole. Since then, the river flows have been dropping rapidly, with my favorite time of the whole fishing season coming these next few weeks.

Still, I'll remember that outing as one of the highlights of the year, and one of my personal good old days.

Golden Years, Golden Hours

Chapter 9

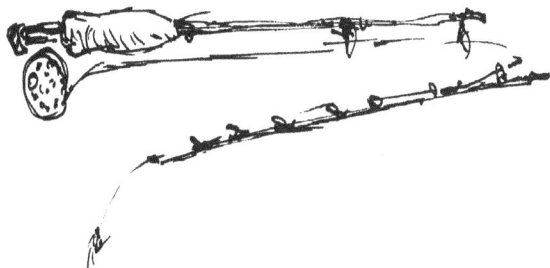

Practicing for Patagonia

I like to think of the Big Hole as my "home water," but I often fish other waters, as well, especially the Madison River. The lower Madison, below Ennis Lake, is a favorite destination for winter and spring. In summer months, when the lower Madison gets too warm for fishing, the upper Madison is a good choice. There are many access points and campgrounds along the river, making it a good destination for weekend getaways.

One thing about the Madison to keep in mind, however, is that the wind blows. Then it'll sometimes pause to take a step back and catch its breath to really blow. Perhaps it doesn't blow on the same scale as in the Paradise Valley, but it doesn't have to apologize to anybody.

A couple weeks ago we hauled our trailer to the Madison, south of Ennis. The wind was blowing when we set up camp in the evening, and the wind, howling through the night, rocked the trailer as we tried to get to sleep.

In the morning, the winds subsided a bit as I walked down to the river for a morning of fly-fishing. In fact, for a while the breeze came out of the north, and it actually helped with casting flies upstream. That was a temporary aberration. Soon, the wind switched back to the south and casting into the wind became an act in futility.

I had hoped the winds would die down in the evening, but that wasn't the case, though I had good luck fishing little pheasant tail nymphs on a swing cast, casting across the current and letting the current swing the fly through the water. It's a simple but effective technique that has caught a lot of fish over the years.

The next day we loaded my pontoon boat in the truck and my wife drove me upriver so I could float and fish back to camp. The wind was blowing so hard it was impossible to cast into the wind, though when floating, the motion of the boat effectively neutralized the wind so it was possible to cast. Keeping the boat under control while fishing was something else, however. I finally quit fishing and just enjoyed the boat ride. It was a quick trip.

The winds kept blowing, bringing afternoon thunderstorms that cleared the air but didn't slow the winds that howled through another night.

Still, miracles can happen. On the last morning of our weekend we awoke to unexpected silence, other than the sound of the river. The winds had died down in the early morning and it was possible to simply go outside without getting blown over or seeing your hat go sailing off toward Ennis. Casting a fly into the river that morning was relatively effortless—even pleasurable.

Even when the winds die down, fishing the Madison is still a challenge. The 50 Mile Riffle, as it's often called, is a big, brawling river that's hard on boats and it's hard on wade anglers. The wind may occasionally subside but the river keeps right on going and if an angler gets dumped, things can get dicey in a hurry.

But, there is the fishing, and it makes it worthwhile. The river has its secrets, though it occasionally gives rewards. I've caught nice fish on the river over the years. I didn't catch any trophy fish that weekend, but I can't help but wonder about the trout that sipped in a little Humpy fly and casually demonstrated significant strength as it headed off into the main current of the river before it popped a poorly tied tippet knot.

That might have been the best fish of the year, I thought sadly, as I reeled in my line.

A dream fishing trip, for many, might be the Patagonia regions of Argentina and Chile. It's still just a fantasy for me, but if I ever go, I can say I've had practical experience for coping with the legendary winds of Patagonia. I've fished the Madison.

Chapter 10

Dangerous Wildlife

A late August day on the lower Big Hole River. The river bottoms were full of grasshoppers and the trout were feasting. In mid-afternoon the fish quit biting so I called it a day and trudged back to where I'd parked that morning. A pickup camper was parked next to my truck.

At the camper was a couple from Germany, where they were members of a fly-fishing club. They had flown to Salt Lake City, rented the RV and headed for Montana. They spotted my truck and figured if locals fish here it must be good, and waited for me to come back so I could tell them about the fishing.

We chatted about fishing and flies, and I showed them the hopper patterns that I used that day.

Then the man asked, "Is there wildlife out there?" gesturing toward the river.

"There are lots of birds," I said, adding, "I frequently see deer. I saw a bull moose this morning."

"Are there any bears?"

"No, I've never seen a bear in this area," I assured him. Evidently that was all he was worried about. He finished gearing up and strode off into the brush.

A couple minutes later, with a frantic look on his face, he came back at a dead run.

Bears? Forget bears. Mosquitoes are the wildlife to worry about.

Golden Years, Golden Hours

Chapter 11

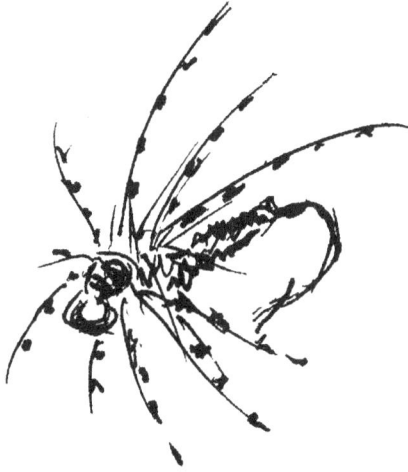

A Baker's Dozen

Like a squadron of kamikazes, the mosquitoes buzzed around, making suicide attacks as I trudged through the river bottom brush. I quickened my pace, hoping to get to my fishing spot with only minor damage. Big Hole River mosquitoes are a hardy breed. They have a lot of work to do in their two-month season, and if they're going to perpetuate the species they have to find victims and suck a little blood before they lay their eggs and start another generation of mosquitoes.

I finally got to my destination: a long riffle and pool on the inside curve of a river bend. It's a magical place that has provided many enjoyable evenings in previous seasons. It was my first visit this year and I wondered if the fish would be hungry, and if so, for what. My

Lab Flicka wasn't worried about fishing. She was with me and able to play in the shallow waters or in the brush next to the river, so she was happy.

I studied my flies, wondering which would be productive. I selected a beadhead, soft-hackled pheasant tail nymph, a favorite fly for evening fishing.

I mused about how my fishing habits have changed over the years. I used to think of myself as a dry fly purist, but those days are over. Using a wet fly is a relaxing way to fish. Instead of having to pick out the drift of a dry fly in the evening glare, I just cast across the current and let the fly swing across. If a fish is going to hit I'll feel it, and more often than not, the hit will come at the end of a swing. If, after a cast or two, I don't get a hit I'll take a step or two downstream and start again.

At first I didn't get any action and I wondered if I should try a different fly. Then I felt the tug of a fish at the end of my line. It didn't take long to bring in the six-inch brown trout, or the next yearling that came a moment later.

Then I had a strike from a fish that had a lot more muscle behind it. My reel screamed as the fish tore down the river. A few minutes later the fish tired and I slid it into the shallows to unhook it, a brown trout of around 17-inches.

I caught a couple more browns of around 15-inches shortly after that, and I began to look at my watch. I planned to fish until 9 p.m. so that I could bushwhack through the brush, weeds and fallen trees back to camp before it got too dark. I thought, *It would be nice if I could get ten fish before 9:00.*

I caught a couple rainbow trout that amused me with their acrobatics and then another yearling brown trout. At 8:50 I had ten trout, so I figured I'd better raise my goals. Let's make it a dozen before 9:00.

The fish kept cooperating and at 8:59 I had a dozen trout, so I raised my goal another notch. Can I catch another trout in the next minute to make it a baker's dozen?

I'll confess my watch had just blinked past 9:00 when I made my last cast and hooked yet another fish. I let the fish go, wound in my line and hooked my fly, the third beadhead, soft-hackled pheasant tail nymph of the evening, on the hook-holder. The fly was falling apart but it had done its job and we had our baker's dozen, nine brown trout and four rainbow trout, for the evening session.

There isn't much logic to this fishing, I thought, as Flicka and I braved the mosquitoes. Earlier, during the morning and afternoon, I had put in a seven-hour float on the river fishing some of the prettiest water in Montana, catching three or four small fish. Now, in one relaxing hour, I had my most productive fishing of the year.

No there isn't much logic—or justice, either, to fishing, but if we put in our time on the river, occasionally the fish gods will bless us.

Golden Years, Golden Hours

Chapter 12

A Love for Soft-Hackles

The sun was dropping as I waded into the pool on the Big Hole River. Caddisflies were buzzing around, along with various midges and other tiny bugs, looking almost more like motes of dust than insects. An occasional mayfly would also take wing into the fading sunlight.

With the variety of bugs on or near the water's surface, as well as diminishing light, trout began feeding along the water's surface. What were they feeding on? Hard telling. I tried a couple different dry flies, but if the fish liked them or not, it was hard to tell because of glare on the water, or, looking in another direction, too little light to see what was happening.

That meant it was time to change tactics and tie on one of my go-to flies: a soft-hackled wet fly.

The soft-hackled fly is one of our oldest styles of fly patterns, originating centuries ago in England. When you look at a soft-hackled fly for the first time you'd likely think, as I did years ago, "They don't look like much." You'd be right; there isn't much to a soft-hackled fly. It's simply a small hook, such as a #14 or 16 dry fly hook, with a sparse body of silk floss or dubbing, with a couple turns of partridge hackle at the front.

Still, we aren't the best judges of what looks good when it comes to trout flies. It's the trout's opinion that counts most. This evening, the trout thought soft-hackled flies looked like food. My first strike came from a 15-inch brown trout that went speeding down the river after it felt the sting of the hook. After I released the trout, more fish took the fly, including a couple that felt heavier and stronger than that first brown trout, though they got off before I had a chance to identify them. I landed a couple more browns and a nice rainbow before failing light and dropping air temperature persuaded me it was time to call it a night.

The next morning I chatted with Brian and Pat from a neighboring campsite, and told them about catching fish on soft-hackled flies. They said, "What kind of fly is that?" I really didn't have time to explain the concept, as they had to run to meet a guide for a float trip on the river. That afternoon I tied a few soft-hackled flies for them and explained how to fish with them. It's easy. Just cast the fly across the stream and let it drift down and swing across the current, and keep a light setting on the reel's drag, so you don't break a tippet when fish hit.

I omitted the more detailed history of soft-hackled flies and how one person almost single-handedly is responsible for the modern resurgence of these simple fly patterns. Sylvester Nemes, who lived in Bozeman, Montana in his later years, wrote the book *Soft-Hackled Flies* in 1975. He followed that book with *The Soft-Hackled Fly Addict and Soft-Hackled Fly Imitations*, plus several others in later years.

Nemes was a guest speaker at a local Trout Unlimited meeting in 1998 and I had an opportunity to interview him the next day, and even spent an afternoon fishing with him a few weeks later. Syl served in the Army Air Corps during World War II and was stationed in England, where he met Hazel, his English war bride. He also had the opportunity to fish English trout streams where he first learned about soft-hackled flies.

Syl died a few years ago, though he'll long be remembered for his thoughts and writings about fly-fishing.

That evening I returned to the river and the fish were all over my soft-hackled fly. In a 50-minute session I caught and released a dozen fish, about half rainbows and browns plus a couple humongous whitefish.

The next morning I asked our new friends if they fished that evening. They reported almost sensational fishing success using soft-hackled flies. As I told my wife, "I think I've got a couple new converts to soft-hackled flies."

Which reminds me; I need to tie some flies, not to mention try to get a couple Hungarian partridge this fall. It's where flyfishing and upland bird hunting meet and merge into one.

Golden Years, Golden Hours

Chapter 13

Murder on the Madison

It was clearly a case of murder.

The victim's eyes had long ago glazed over and the body had passed through rigor mortis and lay limply on the grass.

It wasn't your ordinary homicide—where the perpetrator checks for valuables and moves on. The perp not only committed violent murder; it stayed to feast on the victim.

I asked my wife, a connoisseur of murder mysteries, "Friend of yours?"

"Never saw him before," she said. Likely story, for first thing she said, "Let's throw the body in the river, before the dog eats what's left of him."

I thought she had spent a little too much time out in the sun, or the last snowstorm of May had affected her reasoning. It's not like her to disturb a crime scene. Certainly, none of the crime-solving heroines of her mystery novels would have suggested that we simply throw the victim of violent death in the river.

"Oh well, 'In for a penny, in for a pound,' as the saying goes." I picked up what was left of the mortal remains and pitched it into the swift waters of the Madison River and watched it float off in the current.

A dead bird's body doesn't weigh much, especially after it has been eaten. It wouldn't take long before other critters would finish the few scraps of meat left on the skeleton; a good snack for a crayfish.

Identifying the deceased bird turned out to be easy. It was about the size of a small duck, but with its long legs, black and white wings, cinnamon-brown head, and a long, pointed beak with a pronounced upturn, it was logical to look in the "sandpiper-like birds" section of the bird book. After looking at just a few pages of photos we made a positive identification of the murder victim. It was an American avocet.

The bird book describes the American avocet as a large shorebird, with its long legs and long up-turned bill as distinguishing characteristics. It breeds along marshes and lakes in intermountain areas of the West and on prairie lakes from Oklahoma to the Dakotas. They make their living by eating shrimp-like crustaceans they catch by sweeping their bill through the water.

We had made a positive ID on the murder victim. The next question was, "Who perpetrated the 'offing' of this seemingly innocent shorebird?"

We ruled out revenge on the part of the avocet's own victims. They may have had ample motive but would have lacked means and opportunity.

From the appearance of the crime scene, with a pile of feathers neatly off to the side of the body, with the breast meat picked cleanly from the skeleton, the perp was likely another bird—a predatory bird.

I didn't have far to look for a likely suspect. While fishing along the river the next day I spotted a bald eagle perched at the top of a dead cottonwood tree. "You the one that bumped off that avocet?" I asked.

The eagle gave me a blank look and flew off. Obviously I was going to get the perp into custody if I was going to get a straight answer out of him.

The next day I saw a shadow move across the river and I looked up to see the eagle fly over, this time flying to another cottonwood tree, where it was greeted by another white-headed bird. "Hmmm, it gets more interesting all the time," I said to myself. "Now we have two suspects."

I climbed the tree and confronted them. "I charge you with the murder of an American avocet. Now, what do you have to say for yourselves?"

The female eagle looked ready to come across with a tearful confession, but the male eagle snarled at her, "Shut up, sister. I'll handle this."

He looked at me with those beady eyes of his and said, "Yeah, I did it. So what? That avocet was too dumb to survive. Furthermore, he didn't even taste that good." He burped unconvincingly and then concluded his statement. "Besides, my legal adviser," he glanced at a raven in a nearby tree, "tells me it was all perfectly legal. We call it 'making a living and supporting a family.'"

He had me there. I walked back to camp and filed my report. It was an open and shut case but I had to let him go on a technicality. If it's legal, it isn't murder.

Case closed.

Golden Years, Golden Hours

Chapter 14

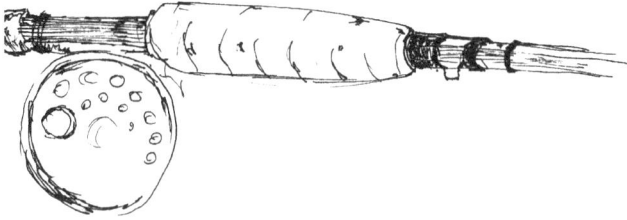

Winning the One Fly Contest

I entered a "One Fly" contest last weekend.

It wasn't the well-known one fly contest. There has been an annual One Fly event at Jackson Hole, Wyoming since 1985. The Jackson Hole One Fly event is an annual fundraising affair where people pay big bucks to enter a contest where they fish the South Fork of the Snake River for two days.

There are forty teams of four people who float the river with local guides who also act as referees. Anglers win points by landing trout (whitefish don't count), which are measured before release. Prizes are awarded to high scoring teams. The catch to the whole process is that anglers get to use just one fly for the weekend. They can fix it with Super Glue if it starts falling apart, and if they hook a tree and break off, they can retrieve the fly and keep on using it—if they can retrieve it safely, as judged by the guide. On the other hand, if the angler loses the fly, whether to a fish or a snag, that person is out of the contest. Anglers in this contest use flies and tippets made to be durable, as they don't want to break off and have to drop out.

In recent years, the event has raised over $100,000, which is used for conservation projects in the South Fork watershed.

My One Fly event was not by intention but one of those senior moments.

We were camping on the Big Hole River and after a leisurely breakfast, I put my pontoon boat in the water for a three-hour float to a downstream bridge.

I floated through some quiet water and then pulled over to fish a riffle about half a mile downstream from the launching point. I sensed an unexpected feeling of lightness and freedom, when I suddenly realized it was because I'd left my vest back in camp. All I could do at that point was laugh at my predicament. I did have a fly on my line: a tiny size 18 bug I used to catch some whitefish the previous evening. That fly was tied to a wispy 5X tippet.

In the game of flyfishing, flies are the pawns. We buy or tie them by the dozen and we expect to change them if they don't produce, and if we lose them we shrug and tie on another.

If I were planning to use just one fly for several hours of fishing I wouldn't have chosen that tiny dry fly. In the heat of the day, nothing was hatching and fish weren't rising. I could have walked back to camp to retrieve my vest, but that would have been a half hour walk through the brush and mosquitoes and another half hour back. That wasn't a good alternative, so I figured my best bet was to fish with what I had and hope I didn't snag something and lose my fly. I wanted to be a player, not a tourist.

In that first riffle I did catch and release a ten-inch brown trout. Then I re-launched to drift down to the next riffle. A kingfisher flew by and landed in a nearby tree. Kingfishers don't worry about losing flies or breaking tippets.

In the next riffle I caught and released a whitefish. I hooked some grass on a backcast, but didn't break off. Moving to another riffle, one fish took a brief look at my fly before deciding it was a fake. I picked up several aluminum cans from the riverbed that slobs had discarded.

The take-out point was in sight when I made my last stop. I was getting some bumps and nibbles on my fly, which was a chewed-up wet fly by then. Storm clouds were building and fat rain drops were falling as I approached the bridge, changing to hail as we loaded the boat into the back of the truck.

The float trip was a private game of Survivor—the goal was to stay in the game to the end—and not have to finish the float as a tourist. I finished as a winner.

Golden Years, Golden Hours

Chapter 15

A Modern Parable

In 1992 I built a 7- foot, 9-inch 2-weight fly rod from a G. Loomis blank. I know some people don't like ultra-light fly rods, but that fairy wand of a fishing pole has been a favorite fishing tool. After using it for about five years, the tip section broke while I was playing a fish. I told my sad story to the company and they sent me a new blank.

A few years ago, I carelessly closed a car door on my rod and broke the tip. Believe it or not, the people at G. Loomis sent me another new blank, though this time for a 3-weight rod, as they had discontinued that particular rod blank in the 2-weight version. I built my new 3-weight rod, but also fitted a new tip-top to my car-shortened rod and kept using it.

On an August outing, my son, Kevin, and I floated the Big Hole River in our pontoon boats. A few miles downstream from Melrose we pulled in to shore for wade fishing and a lunch break. When we re-launched I put the rod in its holder and pushed out. When I launched, the rod bounced out of the holder and was swept away in the swift river currents. We searched as best we could but the rod disappeared. It was a melancholy float back to camp that afternoon.

While I was sad about losing my pet rod, I couldn't complain. That little rod and I had teamed up to catch a lot of fish for almost 20-years.

Sometimes, however, sad stories have happy endings.

A month later I again floated that section of the river and stopped at the place where the rod went for a swim and started a new search. The river had dropped over the last few weeks and maybe I might find it this time—and find it I did.

It had washed up in the shallows less than 100 yards from where I lost the rod. It was somewhat the worse for wear from spending almost a month in the river. Everything that could catch moss did catch moss. The finish on the reel and on metal parts was tarnished. The varnish on the rod windings was discolored and likely deteriorated. Nothing good happens when you throw a fishing pole in the drink.

Still, aside from cosmetic issues, the rod was intact. The reel, while tarnished, worked perfectly. There was still a fly at the end of the leader, though the point of the hook had rusted away.

I would have a winter project to thoroughly clean up those metal parts, along with stripping off the guides and, essentially, rebuild the rod.

If that float back to camp a few weeks earlier had been a sad voyage, this time it was festive. Not much could have destroyed my good mood. In addition, the fish were biting. The only thing I lacked was a bottle of bubbly with which to celebrate the day.

In the Bible, Jesus tells the parable about the shepherd rejoicing after finding a lost sheep. I know how he felt.

That fly rod had a long history, and with a little bit of luck the saga continues.

Still, one lesson I'd best not forget is that if your boat's rod holder has a Velcro strap, it's probably there for a reason.

Golden Years, Golden Hours

Chapter 16

Milo Goes Fishing

Milo was sitting at the bar nursing a beer. I took the stool next to him and ordered a bump and a beer for each of us. He tossed back the shot and half the glass of beer and said, "Thanks, but what's goin' on?"

I sipped my beer and said, "Your buddy, Rick, said you'd been down in the dumps. Said you wanted to go fishing."

"Yeah…so what?"

"So what is I'm going down to the Big Hole tomorrow. You comin' or not?"

"You drivin'?"

"You betcha, I'll pick you up at 8 a.m.—that is if you think Hazel will let you go."

"Let me? Just watch, she'll lock the door behind me so I don't change my mind. Oh, if you're drivin' I'll bring lunch,"

I finished my beer and as I headed for the door I heard Milo call my name. I turned and Milo said, "Hey kid, don't be late."

The sun had just risen over the East Ridge when I pulled up in front of Milo's house. He walked down the sidewalk and threw hip boots and a beat-up old rod case in the back of my truck, along with a cooler. Then he said, "Pop the hood, please."

He took two foil-wrapped packages and nestled them on top of the engine block. "Lunch," he said. "Hazel made pasties last night. They're cold now, but after driving down to the river and sitting on top of the engine all morning, they'll be piping hot at noon."

45 minutes later we pulled in to the fishing access. With our early start we had the river to ourselves. We got out of the truck and walked down to the river. I could see some PMDs coming off the river and I said, "Hmmm, there are some *Ephemerella Infrequens* hatching this morning."

"Yeah," said Milo. "And there's some little yellow bugs, too."

We returned to the truck and began gearing up. I was wading wet today, so I just had to take off my shoes and put on some wading boots. Milo tugged hip boots on over his blue jeans. "I just bought these last night. Spent 30 bucks for them, so they oughta be good." I raised my eyebrows but didn't say anything. The last time I wore rubber-soled hip boots in the Big Hole I went for a swim in the middle of the river.

I assembled my G. Loomis 2-weight graphite rod. Milo opened his battered rod tube and pulled out a three-piece bamboo rod. It was a vintage Orvis rod. "I've had this a long time. Spent a hundred bucks for it back in '48. Good thing I wasn't married yet. Hazel would have skinned me alive."

I agreed that some things were better left unsaid. I tied a #18 PMD pattern on my 5X tippet, and asked Milo, "What are you using?"

Milo pulled a George Grant Black Creeper from his hatband and said, "Same as I always use. I bought a dozen of these when George still had his shop on Harrison. 80 cents apiece I paid for 'em. You'd think he would have given me a discount for buyin' them by the dozen. I'll bet he made millions on them flies of his."

"I don't know about that, Milo. The way I heard it, he just made a lot of flies. I've got a few of them too. The Chamber of Commerce office was selling them for $10 apiece."

"Ten bucks! Man, they sure saw you comin,' didn't they."

All geared up, we split. Milo went upstream and I went down. We agreed to meet back at the truck at noon.

I had a good morning. Browns and rainbows, not to mention a ton of whitefish, were rising to the mayflies. I caught and released a half dozen fish, including an 18-inch brown trout. I saw Milo walking to the truck. His wicker creel was hanging heavy at his hip, with six inches of fishtail hanging out the top. Milo was grinning. "That big Loch took that ol' Creeper like it was a pasty. Guess what we're having for supper tonight?"

Milo took a six-pack from his cooler and gently laid the big trout on ice. We got the pasties from under the hood and sat at a picnic table and had our lunch. "Mighty good, Milo," I said. "Wish you'd remembered the gravy, though."

Milo laughed sheepishly. "Yeah, yeah. I'll get after Hazel about that." He looked at the river, sparkling in the sun. "That was a good morning. We'll have to do this again."

Author's note: Rick Foote was a continuing presence as a reporter, editor and columnist in newspapers in Butte, Montana from the 1960s until his death in 2013. A recurring character in his columns was a crusty old-timer, Milo the Miner. Occasionally, Rick might throw in a reference to my outdoor columns and Milo feeling down because he hadn't been fishing.

George Grant was a much-honored and beloved fly-tyer, conservationist and writer. He developed and patented a style of hair-hackled flies, of which the Black Creeper was best known. In his later years he founded the Big Hole River Foundation, and in his 90s, tied flies to be sold at the Butte Chamber of Commerce to raise money for the foundation. Trout Unlimited recognized Grant as one of the organization's heroes of TU's first 50 years, and the Butte chapter of TU is named in his honor. He died in 2008 at age 102.

When brown trout were introduced in Montana the fish were supposedly from a strain of brown trout from Loch Leven in Scotland. Lots of old-timers still refer to brown trout as "Lochs."

And pasties? Pasties (not to be confused with pastys) are a piecrust filled with meat and potatoes, and baked to a golden hue. Their origin is in the Cornwall area of England. Cornish miners came to many mining areas in the U.S. during the 1800s, and wherever they settled they left their culinary legacy of pasties.

Golden Years, Golden Hours

Excursions

Golden Years, Golden Hours

Chapter 17

The Trouble with Travel

I don't have the travel "bug."

I know people who do have that travel bug and look forward to traveling the world. One couple, close friends from our former home in North Dakota, has become globetrotters in recent years, and there aren't many places in the world worth visiting that they haven't been to.

I envy them—a little. I've been fortunate to see much of the U.S. I've had gumbo and jambalaya on a restaurant's balcony in New Orleans' French Quarter, after fishing coastal waters in the morning. I've been to Disneyland. I've been in our nation's capitol and experienced the sudden hush when you enter the Lincoln Memorial. I've witnessed the Changing of the Guard at the Tomb of the Unknowns in Arlington National Cemetery. That visit included stop at a peaceful hillside in a secluded corner of Arlington National Cemetery that, just a couple years later, became the site where an eternal flame marks the resting place of John F. Kennedy.

It's good to travel and to walk along the paths of history.

The biggest problem with travel is that to do it you have to travel.

Travel is, in many respects, easier than it used to be. When my father, who was born in 1900, was a boy growing up in Norway, cross-country skis were basic winter transportation. At age 17 he crossed the Atlantic on a steamship and came to the Midwest by train, in an era when you could literally go anywhere by train.

A few decades earlier, traveling the west meant journeys measured in months. From our 21st Century standards of comfort and convenience, it's inconceivable to put ourselves in the place of people who set out in wagons to travel the Oregon Trail. Even more intriguing was the period when families traveled the Mormon Trail hauling all their possessions in handcarts—glorified wheelbarrows.

Yet, historians who have studied the journals of these pioneers point out that a surprising aspect of these travel experiences is that, for many, it was the most free and relaxed period of their life. Settlers on the edge of the frontier seldom enjoyed leisure. Yet, on the trail, they had hours and hours of time when they could let their minds wander or just mount a horse and go hunting or exploring.

These days we can hop on a jet and in a few hours, if all goes well, be almost anywhere. That is, if all goes well.

Delays seem to be the norm. On one trip we checked in well ahead of time only to learn our flight was going to be delayed an hour and a half late due to "mechanical difficulties." We eventually made it to Seattle, just to learn that our connecting flight was cancelled due to mechanical difficulties. This all translates to sitting in an airport for hours at a time.

Architects and planners strive to make big city airports efficient. What they actually achieve are depressing tunnels where prisoners serve indeterminate sentences, forced to walk briskly with confused looks on their faces.

There are variations among the prisoners. You can spot the business travelers, with cell phones attached to their ear as they check in with their office. There are older travelers, many of whom don't often travel and expect the worst to happen. In their one and only commercial airline trip, my wife's parents struggled to get everything they could possibly need into carry-on bags. "You hear about people's luggage getting lost or sent to the wrong city," my mother-in-law explained, "and there's no reason it can't happen to us."

Meanwhile, back in our Seattle prison, I grow weary and shut my eyes to attempt a nap, ignoring the parade of prisoners walking the halls. With my eyes shut, noise dominates the senses. It's an endless monotony of announcements of flights boarding, smoking rules, don't leave your car unattended, scraps of conversation from passersby. Somewhere, from a distant television, there's a report of heavy snow on the East Coast.

Eventually, problems are resolved. We escape from prison and arrive at our destination. The next day we're in the Napa Valley, sipping incredible wine and chatting about viticulture and crop yields. It runs about 230 cases of wine per acre, by the way.

It's a great thing to travel and experience things. It's too bad we have to travel to get there.

Golden Years, Golden Hours

Chapter 18

Be Prepared!

After a conference at Social Security headquarters in Baltimore, Maryland, I was at Baltimore-Washington International airport, checking in for the first leg for the trip back to Montana.

The agent kept checking and rechecking something, so I finally asked, "Is there a problem?"

"Yeah, your airplane for Minneapolis hasn't left Minneapolis yet."

Obviously, if your first flight is hours late, you're going to be late getting home. The agent kept checking his computer and finally said, "There's a 4:30 flight to Minneapolis leaving from National. I can get you on that flight." (Note: this was before National was renamed Ronald Reagan National Airport.)

It was 3 p.m. when he finished booking me on that flight. He gave me a voucher for a cab ride to Washington D.C. and suggested I'd better hurry up and get going.

I ran out with my suitcase and hailed a cab and we hit the road for D.C., and made good time, going by the National Security Agency and other government installations and then getting to D.C. just in time for Friday afternoon rush hour.

Still, the cabbie got me to the terminal before the plane took off and I somehow made it through the boarding process with a couple minutes to spare, and, thankfully, settled into my seat in the last row of the plane, wondering who would be coming to the vacant aisle seat next to me.

The last person to board, just before attendants shut the cabin door, came down the aisle and, with a look of relief, exhaled and sat down next to me.

As the plane flew over the eastern half of the United States, we chatted about what we did, and where we were going. I was a manager for the Social Security Administration heading back home to Montana. He was a documentary filmmaker, he explained, flying to Minneapolis where he was going to film a political candidate in action, the first step in creating what would become a television commercial.

I had lots of questions about his work as a filmmaker, as he talked about the many types of films he'd worked on.

He reflected that the most interesting experience he'd ever had was a missed opportunity. He lived in Washington D.C. and one pleasant summer day, he didn't have anything scheduled. "My cameraman and I decided to go out to National Zoo and try to get some stock footage of the zoo and people enjoying the summer day.

"About noon, we sat down on a park bench, across from a chimpanzee enclosure, for a lunch break.

"While we were sitting there, eating our sandwiches, a mother with a couple kids, African-American for whatever it's worth, came along. One of the kids, a little girl, was carrying a bag of Oreo cookies. On an impulse, the girl took a cookie and walked up to the cage and handed a cookie to a chimp. The chimp took the cookie and carefully twisted it into its two halves, then licked the frosting off, before eating the two cookie halves.

"Then my cameraman and I looked at each other with this expression of, 'Did you see what I just saw? That'd be worth millions.'"

But, it wasn't to be. They introduced themselves to the family, who agreed to work with them. "We went through the rest of that bag of cookies," he reminisced, "but we could never recreate that scene.

"It certainly proved, however," he continued, "that you never know when the opportunity of a lifetime is coming your way, and you'd better be ready."

Chapter 19

Duck Soup

"Easy as duck soup."

That generally means something that is easily accomplished, though if you do an Internet search of "duck soup" you'll likely get more references to the 1933 Marx Brothers movie of that name, along with some recipes.

If you ask a mama duck what she means by duck soup you may get a totally different answer. In late June, while attending a conference in Bismarck, North Dakota, I took advantage of a Ducks Unlimited field trip to take a look at a tract of land DU acquired the previous year, and, incidentally, keeps open for public hunting. The property is relatively pristine prairie in the Missouri Couteau area of central North Dakota.

The Missouri Couteau is a vast area extending from central Saskatchewan, going south across northeastern Montana and through the Dakotas. It's an area marked by rolling prairie, and most importantly, as far as ducks are concerned, many wetlands scattered across the prairie.

Glaciers formed the Couteau 10,000 years ago. As the glaciers stalled out and melted, the ice sheets dumped vast amounts of debris they'd carried across North America, forming the hilly, rolling landscape. Through the centuries the prairie became home to bison, elk, deer, sharp-tailed grouse and, of course, waterfowl.

DU biologists explained the property's features, though one of the more fascinating demonstrations was of the hidden life within the wetlands and its importance to waterfowl. A biologist at Ducks Unlimited's regional headquarters in Bismarck filled containers with pond water from a couple nearby wetlands.

It's a complex slice of life, with a whole predator/prey system of its own. Some of the wildlife captured in a couple water buckets included bloodworms, caddisfly larvae, mosquito larvae (hatching into adult mosquitoes before our eyes), freshwater shrimp, dragonflies and damselflies, mayflies, tadpoles and leeches. A close look at one small beaker of water showed a tiny little red round bug, a seed shrimp, in constant motion, buzzing around its underwater environment.

As summer progresses, various forms of invertebrates emerge and become active. It's an environment tailor-made for ducks. When ducks migrate north in the spring they'll feed in the prairie wetlands. In early spring, not much is active other than snails, which give ducks a good feeding of protein and calcium necessary for developing eggs.

The scattered wetlands are important as mallard hens, for example, will not tolerate other mallard hens along the same wetland, though they will tolerate ducks of other species. Presumably, that's because other duck species have different dietary requirements so their needs aren't competitive. Large tracts of grassland protect duck nests from predators such as skunks and foxes.

While a casual hiker wouldn't likely notice a duck nest, ducks were actively laying and incubating eggs. Nests are nestled into little clumps of grass out on the prairie. After eggs hatch, mama duck leads her brood of baby ducklings up to a mile to wetlands where ducklings dine on their rich diet of duck soup through late summer. At that time dietary needs will shift to seeds and other vegetation.

On a nearby hilltop other wetlands were in view, some nearly dry. It's part of a wet/dry cycle necessary to renew the vitality of the wetlands. It's a process that has been going on for millennia. A range biologist pointed out the many varieties of native prairie grasses and plants in just a small area. DU manages the prairie using cattle grazing, fire, and some chemical control of invasive plants. Their goal is to mimic the processes of natural prairie.

A granite boulder on a hillside indicates how long the process has been going on. The ground around the boulder looks packed down. The ends of the boulder were polished until smooth and shiny. For centuries, bison walked across this hillside, stopping, occasionally, to rub on the boulder to help get rid of their winter coat or just to relieve an itch.

When we again scan the autumn skies for signs of migrating waterfowl, we might pause to consider the complex factors that come together to grow a duck into adulthood. Making duck soup isn't all that easy.

Chapter 20

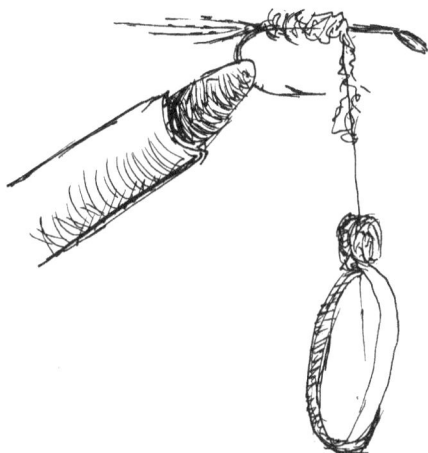

Hexed in Michigan

With the sun just above the western horizon, the shadows are lengthening. The evening air is alive with mosquitoes and black flies. Birds are calling and somewhere in the forest a ruffed grouse is drumming, though for his own amusement, as spring mating season ended weeks ago.

As evening gradually turns to night, the anglers of the Au Sable spread out along the river to stake out a section of water and patiently wait for things to happen. Among those anglers is a visitor from Montana, whose home water, the Big Hole River, still has a remnant population of arctic grayling. I was in Michigan for the annual conference of the Outdoor Writers Association of America, and stayed on for several days of fishing with my friend, Charley Storms, of Evansville, Indiana. We'd been planning this outing for almost a year, after he visited Montana to fish the Big Hole.

The Au Sable is one of America's great trout rivers. It's in northern Michigan, the northern part of the Lower Peninsula, that is, near the town of Grayling, where, ironically, a wonderful arctic grayling fishery was wiped out in the 1800s through logging and over-fishing. When the days of Paul Bunyan and his blue ox, Babe, were over, the forests were gone, the rivers scoured by rafts of logs sent downstream every spring to Lake Huron ports and sawmills to build American cities.

As nature gradually healed the landscape, brook trout and brown trout were introduced to the rivers, and new angling traditions took hold, chief among which is the pursuit of the hex. The *hexagenia limbata* is a mayfly—America's largest mayfly. The hex spends most of its life in silty river or lake bottoms until warm evenings in early summer, when nymphs leave the muddy streambed and emerge to the water's surface for one last glorious moment as an adult winged insect to mate, lay eggs and then die, its life's mission complete—unless a big brown trout intervenes.

In late June anglers converge on Michigan streams such as the Manistee and Au Sable, just as others head to western rivers for the salmonfly hatch. In addition to the hex, there are brown drakes and mahogany duns, other large mayflies with nocturnal habits. While many guides work the waters, we were privileged to tap into a brotherhood of local anglers who daily pass the word around as to where the hatches are happening—especially the hex hatch. Our window into that brotherhood was area resident and new friend, Doug Nagel, a retired teacher and angling fanatic, whose wife, Ginny, not only puts up with his nocturnal wanderings, but reminds him he'd better go yet another night, or he'll regret missing it.

So there we were with Doug and his friend, Steve Beardsley, another local resident, sitting on a log on the bank of the river. We'd taken canoes downstream to get an early reservation for the hatch.

At 10 p.m., it was almost dark and fireflies were blinking in the trees. Doug spotted a mayfly floating down the stream like a miniature sailboat, and then more and more. Like sharks, brown trout came to the surface, attacking and devouring the annual bounty of super-sized mayflies.

"Be ready," Doug coached us visitors. "Watch for the swirls, and you'll know where the fish are." Steve was first to connect. I cautiously stepped into the muddy bottom, not wanting to go for an unplanned swim. I made casts at disappearing rise rings, but that fish quit feeding. "There's another feeding over there," Doug said, "you'd better move."

I stumbled through mud and tangled brush and re-entered the water and resumed casting—now a game of casting in almost total darkness at the sound of feeding gulps. Suddenly, an explosion hit my fly and the fight was on. After a few minutes I landed a fat brown trout of about 17 inches, though in the dark it was hard telling just how large it was. I've caught bigger trout, but never any as exciting.

After an hour of fishing and frustration in the dark, the action stopped. We loaded the canoes and floated downstream, passing anglers with headlamps or flashlights marking their location, optimistically waiting in the midnight gloom for a new feeding frenzy.

Fishing the hex hatch is mysterious, elusive—and unforgettable.

"Here's the key to your room, but the doors aren't locked, and you don't need to lock it either."

That's not the usual advice you get when you check into a hotel or motel, but Rusty Gates wasn't the usual motel operator. Calvin (Rusty) Gates operated the Gates Au Sable Lodge for many years, a combination fly shop, motel and restaurant on the banks of the Au Sable River in northern Michigan. But then Rusty Gates was an unusual person.

I met Rusty when my friend, Charley Storms, and I got together for a week of fishing. Charley had stayed at the lodge previously, and considered it an achievement to get a reservation during the late June "Hex hatch," the annual emergence of giant mayflies synonymous with the Au Sable River.

Rusty Gates was synonymous with the Au Sable River. He grew up fishing on the river. In 1970, his father, Cal, Sr., quit his job as a high school band director to buy the lodge, then called the Canoe Inn. Young Rusty turned the river into his vocation, tying flies and guiding, then taking over the business when his father died in 1983.

Rusty was a moving force in a campaign to establish "catch and release" rules on a stretch of the main stem of the Au Sable River, a piece of river often called, "The Holy Water." It was a divisive issue, to say the least. Various chapters of Trout Unlimited took diametrically opposed positions on the issue. Rusty formed a new organization, Anglers of the Au Sable, and served as its president for many years, eventually winning increased support of the no-kill policy. His new organization took on other issues, such as oil and gas exploration, chemical pollution, and a major expansion in nearby Camp Grayling, Michigan's National Guard training camp.

For those efforts, *Fly Rod & Reel* magazine named Rusty Gates as its "Angler of the Year," in 1995.

Meeting Rusty behind the counter of his fly shop was an opportunity to meet a living legend of flyfishing. Unfortunately, Rusty was involved in another struggle at the time. While he didn't talk about it unless asked, he was going through treatment for lung cancer, making regular trips to a cancer treatment facility in Chicago. When he did talk about it, it was with a note of confidence—he was the veteran of many battles and didn't intend to lose this one.

Rusty lost that fight, at age 54, on December 19, 2009.

Tributes to Gates include this from Eric Sharp of the Detroit *Free Press*: "If you want to experience Rusty Gates' legacy, drive this winter to the Mason Tract on the South Branch of the Au Sable River and snowshoe or ski through the snowy, hushed woods to the banks of one of the least despoiled streams in Michigan.

"Listen to the wind sighing through the pines, the occasional soft 'plop' of a clump of snow falling from a high branch…Then listen to what you don't hear. Drink in the silence when the wind dies…and absorb a solitude than can be experienced in few places in a state with 10 million people…And know that the reason you won't hear the 'tunk, tunk, tunk' of an oil well or smell its rotten-egg odor is largely because of Calvin Gates Jr., a valiant defender of the Au Sable River system…"

Tom Rosenbauer, an author and marketing director for the Orvis Company said, "Of all the strong conservationists in our world, Rusty was one of the toughest. He was tireless, and he was like a missile in his precision and deadly accuracy. Yet he never, ever, wanted credit for anything—just for the various groups he worked with, especially the Anglers of the Au Sable."

Glen Sheppard, an editor of a Michigan conservation newspaper wrote, "Rusty proved that people don't fill their gas tank to fill their fry pan. They put on their waders to nourish their soul."

Requiescat in pace, Rusty. I suspect he didn't have to ask St. Peter for a key, either.

The Au Sable River was the birthplace of Trout Unlimited, formed in 1959 when George W. Mason, president of the Nash Motor Company, predecessor of American Motors, talked to his friend, George Griffith, (creator of the Griffith Gnat fly) about forming an organization, similar to Ducks Unlimited, to benefit trout. Mason didn't live to fulfill this dream but Griffith and master rod maker, Art Neumann, followed through to form the organization, with an initial meeting in Grayling, Michigan.

While Mason didn't live to see the founding of TU he left a priceless legacy, donating a large tract of land along the South Branch of the Au Sable to the State of Michigan. The Mason Tract preserves public access to long stretches of the river, including public hunting, in an area rich in wildlife such as white-tailed deer, wild turkeys, woodcock and ruffed grouse. The Fisherman's Chapel, an open-air sanctuary built in memory of Mason, overlooks the river.

We stayed a few days at another historic facility, Fuller's North Branch Outing Club, a bed and breakfast inn on the North Branch at the rural community of Lovells. In an earlier incarnation it was known as the Douglas House. Back in the days when railroads went virtually everywhere, Lovells was an easy train ride north from Detroit. It was the weekend retreat for automakers such as Henry and Edsel Ford, the Dodge brothers, and Charles Nash. Other guests, according to manager Judy Fuller, included people such as William Durant, founder of General Motors, author Ernest Hemingway, and inventor Thomas Edison, a close friend of Henry Ford.

Ford built a lodge a few miles downstream from Lovells. While the lodge no longer exists, except for a surviving stone chimney, a caretaker's cottage stands a short distance from a public access site.

One of the traditions connected with the Au Sable River is the boat that bears its name. The Au Sable River Boat was developed to transport mail and groceries to lumber camps up and down the river, and later adapted as a fishing boat. A typical version is 24 feet long, with anglers sitting in the front and middle, and handled by a third person sitting in the stern, using either a canoe paddle or pole. Our friend, Doug, built his own riverboat and took us for a float on a stretch of the river. The boat is remarkably stable, has a shallow draft, and is uniquely suited for floating down narrow streams lined with downed trees.

It's unlikely that I'll have an opportunity to return to the Au Sable River, though many memories remain vivid. On one evening, while waiting for the evening hatch, Charley and I shared a pheasant dinner near a patch of wild orchids on a hillside above the stream. As the light faded, a light drizzle started falling. In the forest, ruffed grouse were drumming, and a whip-poor-will began calling. In the warm, humid night air, countless fireflies sparkled in the brush along either side of the stream. The evening was simply pure magic.

The Au Sable is often called "The Holy Waters." It's a river I'll remember the rest of my days.

Chapter 21

Fishing with Optimism

There's no place like home. There's no place like home.

Nope. This isn't some Dorothy and the Wizard of Oz moment. Still, after spending the better part of two weeks going to a conference and then fishing in Michigan, wading into the Big Hole River and casting a dry fly at Montana trout was a vivid reminder that there's no place like home.

After many weeks of high water I'm looking forward to the next couple months and the heart of the fishing season. For the many people who enjoy floating the river in drift boats and rubber rafts, it has been a banner floating season. Now it's time for some serious fishing.

While the salmon fly hatch brings our area a lot of attention, both nationally and internationally, my favorite time to fish area streams is just beginning. There may not be any more giant stoneflies making flights across the waters, but there are caddisflies, mayflies, and several other types of stoneflies.

At least, that's the theory.

Over the last weekend of June, fishing was more an exercise in frustration than a demonstration of flyfishing prowess. One morning was fun, as I caught half a dozen fish in relatively short order, including a grayling—reminding me of fishing, a week earlier, near Grayling, Michigan, where arctic grayling were extirpated over a century ago. Then the action stopped cold. From then until I finally gave up for the day, nothing in my fly boxes held any attraction to the river's trout.

The next day I caught just one brook trout and another grayling—and who knows, it might have been the same one I'd caught the day earlier.

If the fish weren't cooperative, however, I could always rationalize that the fish were still adjusting to lower water flows now that the height of spring runoff was over. Or there was that cold front that was coming in. Or that it was the wrong phase of the moon. If I can't come up with some excuses for not catching fish, I'd might as well just quit fishing, which is a notion I reject, as the best angling outing is the next one I'm planning.

It's in the nature of angling to be an optimist. A practicing psychologist—and angler—Paul Quinnett wrote about that in his 1994 book *Pavlov's Trout*. Quinnett writes, "The most successful fishermen are chronically optimistic. They believe, and I mean *believe*, in their bones, and in spite of the inherent uncertainty of angling, every single cast will bring a strike."

Quinnett adds, "Successful fishermen…keep their hooks sharp, their line in good shape, their muscles tensed for the hit, their landing net at the ready, and their concentration and attention fully focused on what they're doing. For the truly successful fisherman, the glass is not half full. It's filling and about to run over."

Along that vein, have you ever noticed that when you change flies or lures after a spell of not catching anything, how often the first cast with that fresh lure or fly will bring a response from a fish? I suspect it's not just because the fish were looking for that new hook, as much as that when we change flies or lures we have this optimistic feeling that this is just what the fish are looking for, and we may cast just a little better, pay a little more attention, and that translates into fishing action. As the guy says, my glass is filling and about to run over.

So, if I had a couple days of less than spectacular fishing, it just means that banner days are coming, when all the trout will think my flies are candy-coated.

Which brings up one more random thought. When I was a kid, my dad often told me to spit on my worm to make it more attractive to the fish. He's been gone for many years now, but I still can't help but wonder if spitting on his bait was a successful tactic for him because his spit was always flavored with snoose.

I guess I'll never know.

Golden Years, Golden Hours

Chapter 22

New River

The New River is not what it seems. It's actually considered to be one of the world's oldest rivers. From its source in the mountains of North Carolina it flows northward through the southwestern corner of Virginia and on into West Virginia, where it eventually joins another river on its way to the Ohio River, and, of course, the Mississippi and the Gulf of Mexico.

Most streams in Virginia flow east toward the Atlantic Ocean or Chesapeake Bay, so the New River is an anomaly in more ways than one.

I had been in Roanoke, Virginia for an outdoor writers conference and stayed an extra day to take a float trip for smallmouth bass.

Ken Sullins, an equine veterinary surgeon and part-time outdoor writer, also stuck around for some fishing. Our guide was Blane Chocklett, owner of Blue Ridge Fly Fishers in Roanoke, an expert on the smallmouth bass and trout waters of southwest Virginia.

I'd like to brag about all the big fish we caught, but this wasn't the day for it. The week had been hot and muggy, with highs in the 90s. The night before, however, thunderstorms swept through the area— the leading edge of a cold front. One of the facts of fishing I keep re-learning is that fish don't bite on days like this, even if it wasn't much of a cold front by Montana standards. Still, after a couple days of hot, humid weather, a day with clear blue skies, northwest winds and a high of around 80 was a marked change and the fishing suffered.

That's not to say we didn't catch fish. I ended up with something like five smallies that I caught on streamers. In the shallows we occasionally saw bruisers of big fish casually swim away from Blaine's drift boat. Blaine spent a lot of time apologizing about slow fishing when he wasn't struggling with the oars to keep his boat on track and going downstream. Anybody who has floated a Montana River on a windy day knows how that works.

The river flows through an area with high cliffs soaring above the river. While the Virginia river is a lot bigger, it reminded me a lot of Montana's Smith River, which I'd floated a few years earlier.

The day on the river was, in any event, a refreshing change after spending several days in hotel conference rooms. It's always fun to see some new country and I'm betting that these heavily wooded mountains are spectacular during the fall color season.

Chapter 23

Grad School on Silver Creek

It's a stream full of history, with a cast of characters including Nobel Prize winning authors, movie stars and railroad tycoons. Thanks to The Nature Conservancy, it's also a stream that offers ordinary people the opportunity to try their luck at this famous spring creek, which many describe as a graduate school for anglers.

The stream is Silver Creek—just a little way from the famous resort of Sun Valley, Idaho. In fact, Silver Creek's history is an integral part of Sun Valley's history.

More on that in a moment.

At the invitation of Matt Miller, an outdoor writer friend and public relations director for the Idaho branch of The Nature Conservancy, I, along with my son, Kevin, and several others, spent several days trying our luck on Silver Creek.

Trout, we are told, have a brain the size of a pea. For being primitive creatures, they are well educated on Silver Creek. They have to be, as they see thousands of anglers and every kind of fly that they can throw at them. Besides anglers casting imitation bugs, the fish also have to be aware of herons and other predators.

Still, fish thrive in Silver Creek. They feed on a rich diet of aquatic insects, terrestrials, such as grasshoppers and ants, plus the occasional mouse that blunders over the stream bank. They're used to anglers wading clumsily in their midst and, by and large, know the difference between real and fake. E. Donnall Thomas, Jr., a well-known writer, wrote of his visit to Silver Creek in *Northwest Fly Fishing* magazine. After two hours of casting various flies, he caught a 17-inch brown trout. "On Silver Creek," he reported, "this is nothing less than a triumph."

Silver Creek's modern history began in the 1930s, when Averill Harriman, a railroad tycoon, and later a governor, distinguished diplomat, and adviser to presidents, established Sun Valley as a destination ski resort on the route of the Union Pacific railroad. In order to provide recreation attractions for the off-season, he bought up property along Silver Creek and invited celebrities such as Ernest Hemingway and Gary Cooper to come to Idaho and sample the fishing, as well as hunting for pheasants and ducks along the stream.

In the 1960s, the Union Pacific sold Sun Valley, and in the 1970s, it went on the market again. Jack Hemingway, the then-deceased author's son, had settled in the area, and served on the Idaho Fish & Game Commission. Hemingway learned of the impending sale and approached The Nature Conservancy about purchasing the Sun Valley Ranch property on Silver Creek. The Conservancy acquired the property in 1976, and now owns 850 acres along the stream as well as conservation easements on areas not in the Silver Creek Reserve.

Though the Conservancy could probably operate the stream on a pricey pay-to-fish basis, they maintain the Reserve as a public fishing area, open to all comers. They simply require that anglers sign in at the Visitor Center. You might have to walk a little way to find a stretch of stream without other anglers, but wherever you go, you'll find fish. In addition, they offer guided and self-guided nature walks and educational programs. In this green oasis in the high desert of central Idaho it's an area teeming with wildlife.

There are big fish lurking in the gentle waters of Silver Creek. The conversation our first evening revolved around a disagreement about the stream's biggest fish. The guy who caught a 33-inch brown on a mouse pattern figured he had the record fish, though another person asserted that a mouse pattern isn't a legitimate fly, and that his record 31-inch fish was the legitimate record. That set the tone for optimistic thoughts for the weekend's fishing.

So, how did I do? In an evening session after arrival, I came up empty-handed. The next morning I had a couple momentary hook-ups but the fish quickly shed my hook and went their way. That afternoon, while most of the group took a side trip to the Big Wood River, I elected to stay behind to fish the creek. I was rewarded with two 16-inch rainbows that came up to a 'hopper imitation.

The next morning I was striking out during the trico hatch, but then I noticed Pale Morning Dun mayflies floating down the stream's gentle currents. I changed flies and quickly caught a rainbow—almost a clone of the previous day's trout. That was the end of the action—such as it was. I was actually the only person in our group who had any success this morning. Kevin expressed his frustration, "I'm so close to the fish I can hear their mouths opening and closing but still couldn't get a strike."

On some streams, we might have been disappointed with those results. On Silver Creek, we claim victory and put PhD after our name.

Chapter 24

Prince of Wales

"In the unlikely event our flight turns into a cruise, your seat cushion may be used as a flotation device. Brush off the crumbs, put your arms through the straps and paddle to shore. When you get to shore, feel free to keep your cushion as a souvenir of your trip."

If you do much air travel you know that every so often the flight attendant who does the usually boring pre-takeoff messages is a comedian. Still, this comic act might not have been what I wanted to hear before starting a trip involving flying over ocean.

I was one of several outdoor writers invited to take a September Trout Unlimited-sponsored trip to Prince of Wales Island in southeast Alaska. The trip was to be educational—in more ways than planned.

One of the first things about Alaska travel is to stay flexible. The first legs of the trip, to Seattle and then on to Juneau, Alaska, were right on time. In Juneau, however, the connecting flight to Petersburg was about two hours behind schedule. When we finally arrived in Petersburg and went to the office of the seaplane service scheduled to take us to Prince of Wales Island, we were told that their pilots had already put in a day's worth of flight time, so we'd have to wait until morning.

The tourist season was all but over, so we had no trouble getting rooms at the only hotel in Petersburg, an old fishing community with a strong Norwegian heritage.

It's just a half-hour flight from Petersburg to Point Baker, and our destination at Lands End Lodge. The Lodge specializes in do-it-yourself saltwater fishing for salmon and halibut through the summer season. Lodge guests go out in small boats (which in Alaska are referred to as skiffs) and troll the deep and usually placid waters. The previous couple years, however, they've looked at the island's many coastal streams for fly fishing opportunities for trout and spawning salmon to diversify their business.

There is a road system on the island, though we had to take skiffs across a bay to get access to the road where the lodge keeps a couple vans stashed for the season. Once on the road it's a simple matter to drive until we found a stream that looked interesting.

September is the spawning season for pink salmon and the beginning of spawning for Coho (silver) salmon. "The silvers are in," is a rallying cry for Alaska anglers.

On most days, Dolly Varden trout, a member of the charr family and a cousin of the Lower 48's brook trout, provided much of the angling action. In addition we caught rainbow and cutthroat trout, all native to these coastal streams.

While a couple people in the group caught a few silver salmon, most of the fish we caught were pink salmon, though I confess that we weren't often tempted to keep any pinks. As soon as the pinks get in fresh water to spawn they begin to die, as fungal infections start turning their skin blotchy.

"Bread is the staff of life," is a saying most of us learned early in life. In southeast Alaska, however, salmon is the staff of life for the ecosystem, and it's a lesson difficult to ignore.

Salmon, such as those spawned-out pinks at the end of their life cycle, are the basis of life in southeastern Alaska and much of the entire Pacific Coast.

Salmon streams are not a tidy place. Adult salmon return to spawn in their native streams after several years at sea. After spawning, the salmon has completed its life cycle and dies, but not without being recycled. Salmon eggs feed the trout. Bears, eagles and gulls feed on dead and dying salmon and in the natural process spread salmon proteins throughout the ecosystem, growing trees, shrubberies and other vegetation. Deer, songbirds, grouse, and other wildlife thrive in the forests.

When walking at the edge of a stream, the constant odor in the air is of rotting salmon. You're constantly stepping in half-eaten, rotting salmon, or piles of bear poop, which answers the age-old question, "Do bears poop in the woods?" They do, and copiously.

Southeast Alaska is a temperate rain forest, with some 200 inches of precipitation annually. With all that moisture, and soils fertilized with salmon, trees grow big and forest products have long been a big part of the economy, though it's an exploitive system, with a long history of non-competitive bidding, taxpayer-funded road-building and other subsidies.

After a forest has been clear-cut, vegetation grows quickly, and so thickly that it forms an almost impenetrable barrier to wildlife. Scientists figure it takes about 200 years for a clear cut to once again develop the relatively open character of an old growth forest. The subsidies to the timber industry and the environmental damage from clear-cutting the forest were among the reasons Trout Unlimited brought a group of writers here. It wasn't just about fishing.

Still, it's hard to ignore the fact that with vast amounts of water, both on the island and in the ocean, fishing opportunities are virtually unlimited.

Remember the movie, "Planes, Trains, and Automobiles?"

The comedy featured Steve Martin and the late John Candy, as mismatched travelers surviving a series of mishaps in an epic journey to get home for Thanksgiving.

It felt, for a while, like we were a bunch of actors filming a remake of that movie.

Toward the end of our week on Prince of Wales Island it started raining in a serious way. The rain started to filter into the streams, raising water levels. One stream that, on Monday, was shin deep was waist deep by Friday.

We came to Point Baker by floatplane on Monday and the floatplane was scheduled to pick us up on Saturday to take us back to Petersburg where we'd catch planes to start the trip home.

On Saturday, after a night of rain, the area was socked in with fog. No planes were flying anywhere. We got on the phone and rescheduled our flights and then settled in to spend the day watching college football (the lodge had satellite TV). During breaks in the games we'd look outside for a break in the weather. We didn't see any sunshine, though we'd occasionally spot whales cruising off the harbor entrance.

Alaska, incidentally, is paradise for the rabid football fan. Alaska Time is an hour later than Pacific Time, which means on football weekends, pregame coverage for college and NFL games starts early in the morning. You can spend the entire day, from breakfast to bedtime, watching football.

We hoped we'd get out on Sunday, though we were running out of options. The lodge operators were closing for the season and had to be on the road on Sunday afternoon to catch a Monday morning ferry to Ketchikan and the long drive to their home in Idaho.

Sunday dawned gray and rainy. We were still socked in. We had a conference to discuss the situation. We could move to a bed and breakfast facility across the harbor and hope for a Monday plane. The other option was to crowd into one of the lodge's two vans across the bay and drive down the island to catch that ferry. Our group took the larger of the two vans, cramming luggage and bodies into what little space remained after our hosts filled it with their luggage and frozen fish they were bringing home.

First, we had to cross the bay. It had been placid all week, but it was now a wild ocean ride across heavy waves, getting soaked by salt spray and rain.

The road trip down the island went well, including a stop at a river where we had one last crack at salmon just entering the river, fresh from the ocean. If you want to catch pinks at their best, catch them just as they enter the river.

On Monday morning we met our lodge hosts at the ferry terminal and got on board for the voyage to Ketchikan and flights to Seattle and then home. Incidentally, after driving off the sea-going ferry, we drove to another terminal to take a ferry to the airport, on an island on the edge of town, where the famous "Bridge to Nowhere" was going to be built, until the project attracted notoriety as one of the biggest boondoggles of all time.

The crisp, dry mountain air of Montana never felt as good as it did when I got off the plane that night.

It was good to be home, though I won't forget that first lesson of Alaska travel: plan to be flexible.

Golden Years, Golden Hours

Chapter 25

A Whopper of a Story

"I caught a whopper of a smallmouth," I told my wife on my cell phone, letting her know we were on our way home after fishing.

"You mean an official whopper?" She was referring to the North Dakota Game and Fish Department's Whopper Club, a registry of big fish caught in North Dakota. Over the 50 or so years I've fished off and on in North Dakota, I'd often thought it would be fun to catch a fish that could qualify as a whopper. I said it probably wouldn't qualify as an official whopper, but it certainly was my personal smallmouth whopper.

My son, Kevin, and I had spent the day fishing on Lake Audubon, a central North Dakota impoundment, a lake rated by *Bassmaster* magazine as one of the country's top 100 bass lakes (in 2011, 35 people caught Whopper Club smallies on Audubon), and had a great time with smallmouth bass. The bass were in relatively shallow water along shorelines and around islands. I was using a flyrod and casting streamers and used both streamers and lures. Both worked, though for Kevin, lures were easier to handle while driving the boat.

By day's end we'd each tangled into ten or so smallies. Some got away on their own and others we threw back to grow some more. We kept half a dozen bass for fish dinners. Several fish were pretty impressive. My largest measured 19 inches in length and, according to my trusty old De-Liar, weighed four and a half pounds.

After the cooler of fish had been reduced to packages of frozen fillets, Kevin went online to check the State website and announced, "Your fish was a whopper." The Whopper Club minimum size requirement for smallmouth bass is 16 inches and 3.5 pounds. The only thing my fish lacked was a weigh-in on a commercial scale, such as at a grocery store.

The Whopper Club also has a catch & release program, which does not require an official weight, but the angler must certify the fish was released. Releasing into a freezer bag doesn't count.

For the record, the North Dakota record smallmouth bass weighed in at 6 pounds, 13 ounces, and was 19 inches long. Montana's record smallmouth bass, caught in Fort Peck Reservoir in 2002, weighed 6.66 pounds, and was 21 inches long.

Both those state records are midgets compared to the official world record smallmouth bass caught by a D.L. Hayes in Kentucky over 50 years ago. That one weighed 11 pounds, 15 ounces.

There was a possibility of another record smallmouth bass that was caught in 2008 by a Canadian angler, Steven Grail of Arnprior, Ontario. Based on estimates, the fish could have weighed in at over 12 pounds. That will be one of those elusive what-if situations, as Mr. Grail filleted the fish without ever putting it on a scale. In addition, Ontario fisheries biologists would have wanted to do some scientific study to make sure the fish wasn't a hybrid of some sort.

So, because of the intervention of a sharp knife, Steven Grail missed out on a degree of fame and/or notoriety for catching a world record fish.

The holy grail of fish records is the 22-pound, 4-ounce large-mouth bass caught by George Perry of Georgia, way back in 1932. Over the years many anglers have come close to the record, and a couple fish, including one found dead on a shoreline, were larger, but didn't qualify as a fish caught legally by angling.

Perry did have his huge bass weighed on a commercial scale, so the record has endured over these last 80 years, though not without some controversy, in that there was never any scientific corroboration of the fish itself, nor did a taxidermist preserve the fish, as the Perry family had it for dinner.

During the course of the year I spend a lot more time at home in Montana casting little flies for trout. Still, when trout aren't biting, I might daydream about smallmouth bass.

And if there's another whopper, I'll get an official weight before I eat it.

Chapter 26

Fall Chinook

"Paul, you've got a fish on," our guide, Donald Koskela, said, noticing that my rod was bending and jerking. I pulled the rod out of its holder and, sure enough, a fish was doing its best to shed the hook in its jaw. After a short fight I had the fish near the boat. Donald scooped the fish in a landing net and swung the ten-pound Chinook salmon on board.

This outing was part of a short trip to the West Coast. I had a meeting in Salem, Oregon and we made a mini-vacation out of the trip, checking out Long Beach peninsula in Washington, the Evergreen Aviation Museum in McMinnville, Oregon, and tasting wine at several Willamette Valley wineries. As a warm-up to the meeting, my writer friend, G.I. Wilson from Salem arranged an outing with Donald Koskela, owner of Past Time Fishing Adventures. Donald lives in Salem and does most of his guiding on Oregon coastal waters and bays. Another writer, Ron Kerr of Kimberly B.C. joined us.

It was just getting light when we met Donald at the public marina at Newport, Oregon. Don had just gotten back to the marina after setting crab pots out in the bay. Before we did any actual fishing we went back to check the crab pots where he sorted out the first catch, returning female and undersize crabs to the water, and depositing legal-sized male Dungeness crabs in an ice chest.

Our morning routine was to troll herring baits for a while and then go back to check crab pots (actually, they're wire cages baited with chicken). It's not exactly wilderness fishing, as we were trolling along an urbanized waterfront, with dozens of other boats circling the bay trolling for salmon and crabbing.

After several more rounds of crabbing and trolling, Don said, "Paul, you'd better check your line. I think you're hooked on the bottom." I grabbed the rod and felt the moving weight of a large fish. "There's a fish on!" I exclaimed.

"That's going to be a big one," Don said, and asked G.I. and Ron to clear the decks for action. While I thought my first salmon was big, this one pulled out line with authority, and probably panic. When the fish went on a long run, pulling out a hundred yards of line, Don yelled, with several expletives, "He's got a seal chasing him."

We finally worked the fish, minus the seal, back to the boat and Don netted a 26-pound fall-run Chinook salmon—easily the biggest fish of my misspent life.

Around noon, the tide was ebbing, signaling the end of productive fishing, so we pulled the crab pots and headed back to the marina. G.I. and Ron congratulated me on my fishing skill, though it was hard to call it anything but dumb luck. Don had baited the hooks and showed us how to let line out in the water and set the rods in holders while we trolled. We were using the same baits, tackle and technique. Why I caught two salmon, while G.I. and Ron never had a bite, is one of those flukes of fishing, in which luck often trumps skill.

This had been an extraordinary year for fishing. In a twelve month period, I'd fished in Alaska, North Dakota, Virginia, Idaho, Oregon, and, of course, Montana—from coast to coast and high desert to rain forest.

For whatever it's worth, this Oregon outing was the only one when I wasn't fly-fishing. I guess I lost my purist badge, though my wife appreciated fresh salmon fillets in the freezer.

Golden Years, Golden Hours

Critters

Chapter 27

"Don't forget to roll up your windows."

I was attending a concert of early sacred music at the Immaculate Conception church in Butte, sitting next to an old friend, Andrew Scruggs, and his mother.

Andy is a music teacher and band director in Ennis, Montana. After the concert we were chatting and he suggested, "If you're in my neighborhood this summer, give me a call and we'll go fishing."

That's when his mother said, "Don't forget to roll up your windows."

Andy started laughing and I said, "There must be a story there."

Andy related that in the previous fall, he and his dad had gone fishing in the upper Ruby River. "It was about 20 miles above the reservoir and there was nothing out there but sagebrush and dust.

"I'd left the windows open in my Jeep, so it wouldn't get so hot in the car. It was just about sunset when we got back to the car and Dad said, 'Looks like there's a dog in the back seat.' I said, no, can't be.

"We got a little closer and we saw it was a yearling black bear. He was sitting in the back seat and was finishing up the last of the food.

"He'd eaten our sandwiches and candy bars, drank two cans of soda, two packages of ramen noodles that I stash under the front seat for emergencies, and polished that off with a can of engine oil.

"I opened the front door and the bear scampered up to the front seat and jumped out and ran off. Besides eating everything in sight, he'd taken a bite out of the front passenger seat, but that was the only damage."

"You're lucky you got back when you did," I suggested, "before your bear had a roaring case of diarrhea."

"Right," he agreed, as he put on his coat. "And like I said," he added as we left, "be sure to give me a call when you're coming to the Madison."

"Be sure you roll up the windows."

Western Montana is bear country, though, personally, we've never had any bad encounters with bears.

Some years back, when our son Kevin and his wife Jen were new-lyweds, we drove down to the Big Hole River for an evening picnic and some fly-fishing. After dinner, Kevin and I geared up and walked down to the river and were surprised to see an immature black bear on a gravel bar.

The bear was surprised to see us, too, but curious as well. When he saw us, he plopped down on his butt to observe us. He watched for several minutes before getting bored and wandering off.

When we got back to the car, we learned that my wife, Kay and Jen were sitting in the car, as it was getting cool outside, and the little bear walked up to check things out. They were glad they had packed away the picnic things and were in the car.

A few years ago, I was fishing at another spot on the Big Hole and noted a bear warning at the public access. While standing in the middle of the river a little while later, a passing car caught my attention, and then, just below the access road, I saw a black animal running along. At first I thought it was somebody's black Lab, but then realized it was a black bear.

Many years ago, when we were living in North Dakota, just about every summer we headed west to the West Rosebud River in south central Montana to get our annual dose of fly-fishing and mountain camping.

That summer there were bear problems at the upper river Forest Service campgrounds, especially at the popular Emerald Lake campground, several miles upstream from our campground.

We made a special effort that trip to keep a clean campsite and not leave anything out to tempt a wandering bear. Still, one morning while we were l all in bed, we heard a swish of water and clink of bottles from the Styrofoam ice chest we stashed behind our tent trailer. I looked out and saw the rear end of a big black bear waddling down to the next campsite.

We heard later that the people in the pickup camper at the next campsite had a nervous night. They'd grilled steaks on their charcoal grill the evening before. Before going to bed, they brought the grill into the camper with them. The bear could smell the residual scent of grilling steak and spent hours rocking the camper, hoping to get in.

One day, while hunting ruffed grouse in the aspens, Flicka and I were working our way across a wooded hillside toward a creek bottom where I know from previous hunts there's a clump of mountain ash trees, typically loaded with ash berries in early fall.

As we approached the area we started to see splotches of orange pulp on the ground, as well as aspen trees that looked torn up. Flicka was acting nervous, as well. In fact, I'd swear I could feel my own hair standing on end.

I called Flicka to me and we headed in a different direction, away from this hillside seemingly full of bear sign. We're really not in grizzly country, but we are close to the Continental Divide, an ancient migration route for grizzly bears. In fact, that same season there was a report of a hunter coming across a dead grizzly with an archer's arrow in its body in a creek bottom in the same general area where we were hunting.

Every year we spend some time along Montana's Rocky Mountain Front, enjoying our last camping of the season, and hunting pheasants at several farms.

Grizzly bears are occasionally seen in the area, as they wander out from the mountains onto the prairies. Last fall, one of the farmers whose property I hunt said that they had a mama grizzly, with a pair of cubs, hanging around their farm pond, about 100 yards from their house, for several weeks that summer.

A few years earlier, a bird hunter from Alaska, had a nasty surprise when he was charged by a grizzly bear just a few miles from the same farm. The hunter managed to kill the bear with his shotgun, though it was a close call. Unfortunately, the bear was a sow with three cubs. State wildlife biologists tried to capture the cubs, but were unsuccessful. Game wardens found that the hunter's action was justifiable self-defense, though there are other questions.

The farmers were more impressed with the hunter's stupidity than with his shooting. The area where it happened is described as an island of cottonwood trees, brush and berry bushes. According to the state's grizzly bear biologist, it's a haven for grizzlies. There were up to a dozen grizzly beds in the vicinity. In fact, the local newspaper carried a prominent notice warning people about bears in this area, a wooded island in an ocean of grain fields.

The sad part is that the three cubs, a big family for grizzly bears, likely didn't survive. All in all, there was a net loss of four grizzly bears.

In case you're wondering, I do carry pepper spray with me when I'm hunting in bear country. Still, I hope to continue avoiding bears. A 20 or 28-gauge shotgun isn't much defense from a charging grizzly.

Golden Years, Golden Hours

Chapter 28

Bites

"So, I'm crawling down the road, minding my own business, thinking about a nice, fat mouse, when all of a sudden this giant two-leg comes and puts a stick on my neck. I tell him, 'Hey, cut that out.' Then, the first thing I know he's picking me up. I tell you, I'd had it by then. The two-leg left me with a bit of wiggle room and I was able to stretch my neck and jab him with one fang. Boy, he let me go in a hurry."

If rattlesnakes have story time round the campfire when they return to their dens in the fall, this is the story that one rattlesnake can tell his buddies.

The other side of the coin is that the giant two-leg was my son, Kevin.

It was a Friday morning at camp on the Big Hole River, and after a leisurely brunch I'm ready to go fishing. I hear Kevin and his wife, Jen, calling. Kevin has a funny look on his face. He had spotted a baby rattlesnake on the road next to his campsite, and he decided to pick it up to show everybody. As he tells it, "I've been catching snakes since I was a kid, so this should be no problem. Right? I hold down its head with a stick and grab it right behind the head so it can't bite me. Unfortunately, it has just enough flexibility to turn its head and jab one fang into the side of my right thumb, next to the thumbnail."

His immediate reaction is to ignore the bite. "How much venom can a 10-inch snake have, anyway?" He wants to go fishing and this is just a nuisance. My wife and I are in agreement, however, that he needs to get to the nearest emergency room, and fast.

That nearest emergency room is in Dillon, Montana, a little over 20 miles from camp. By the time Kevin and Jen get there, his thumb is swollen to twice its normal size and the area around the puncture site is turning black and he's feeling a lot of pain. "If you want to know how it feels," Kevin explains, "1) Put your finger in a vise and tighten it down until you start to lose circulation and your fingertip starts to swell up, and it feels like your knuckle is being crushed. 2) Leave it there all day."

At first, the nurse in charge of the ER and the doctor on call think Kevin won't need any antivenin as his symptoms are still localized. As the afternoon progresses, his blood chemistry is going crazy, and he has intense pain going all the way up his arm and into his armpit, and he's losing coordination in both hands. They administer eight vials of antivenin, which is all the hospital had on hand. A normal course of treatment is 10 to 20 vials, so additional serum is brought by law-enforcement relay through the night from Missoula and Butte.

By morning, Kevin has had 20 vials of antivenin and the swelling is going down and his blood chemistry is improving. He was feeling well enough to turn on the TV in his room and finds the only interesting program is a National Geographic show about venomous snakes. By early afternoon, his blood chemistry is near normal, so he's discharged from the hospital.

A principal food for rattlesnakes and other snakes is field mice and voles, and in mid-summer the river bottom meadows are full of them. The night before Kevin's bite, near our campfire we heard a sudden squeaking noise in the grass.

We investigated and we saw a garter snake slithering off with a mouse in its mouth.

Much of Montana is rattlesnake country. A couple days before Kevin's incident I had a non-violent encounter with a rattler while walking to one of my Big Hole fishing spots.

On another occasion my hate of knapweed almost got me in trouble. Knapweed is the scourge of the west, as when it gets established it takes over, outcompeting native plants and grasses. While walking to a fishing spot I stopped to pull some knapweed. I'd been working on this patch for a couple summers and it's made a difference.

This time I was reaching toward a knapweed plant next to an old stump when I heard a buzzing noise. I jumped back, then leaned in for a closer look. A rattlesnake was coiled next to the stump, enjoying his spot with dappled sun and shade, making it easy to maintain a comfortable body temperature.

I decided I didn't hate knapweed enough to further disturb this rattler's peaceful morning and went on my way, though that close call haunted me the rest of the weekend.

Like guilt, a rattlesnake bite is a gift that keeps on giving.

A week after Kevin's little adventure, vacation over and back home in Minot, North Dakota, he had an allergic reaction to the antivenin serum. "If you want to simulate the effects of serum sickness," he said, "I recommend that you roll around naked in a patch of poison ivy, which is also full of mosquitoes and black flies. It is truly awful."

Of course, what was almost as bad was explaining, all over again, to another group of medical professionals how he managed to acquire his snakebite in the first place. Kevin was actually a typical snakebite victim. He was young, male, and provoked the bite. A typical element missing in his adventure was alcohol.

Rattlesnakes are in the pit viper family of venomous snakes. There are some 290 species of pit vipers worldwide. There are 17 species of pit vipers in the United States, and are in three basic groups; copperheads, cottonmouths and rattlesnakes.

Pit viper venom is a complex mixture of proteins that act by breaking down blood tissues. When Kevin came into the emergency room his blood clotting factor was similar to that of a heart patient taking anti-coagulants, and got worse from there.

People who live in snake country tend to be careful, always watching the ground for suspicious sights and sounds. Hunting dogs are often at risk, as they're often moving through cover, noses first. A friend from our church told of his Labrador retriever getting bit while hunting sharptails. The dog was pretty sick for a few days but recovered.

Chuck Robbins, an outdoor writer friend in Dillon, Montana, tells of his German wirehair pointer getting bit by a rattler while on a pheasant hunt far from home. Following the bite, Chuck had trouble contacting a local veterinarian until finally catching one at home that night. The vet, who'd evidently heard this story before, growled, "Well, if she ain't dead yet, she's probably gonna live." He was right.

A postscript to this story, which was good for a couple newspaper columns, came several months later, while chatting with a ranching couple while getting hunting permission. The lady said, "You should know that your column about the snakebite went up on refrigerators all up and down this valley, as a warning to our sons about messing with rattlesnakes."

Guess that proves again that old saying that we all have a purpose in life; if nothing else, to serve as a bad example.

Chapter 29

Urban Delicacies

Urban wildlife is often a thorny issue.

Here in Butte, Montana, the occasional moose or black bear wanders into town. Canada geese live here year round, thanks to open water, people who illegally feed them, and lots of irrigated grassy areas, such as golf courses.

In many parts of the country, deer are major problems. The problem of dealing with deer in urban areas can be particularly complex, though deer aren't the only troublesome critter.

Our daughter, Erin, lived for a number of years in a hilly section of Oakland, California and there's a lot of wildlife in those forested hills, such as deer, wild turkeys, bobcats, and, peskiest of all, raccoon, which have been raiding her garbage cans.

Raccoons are an interesting animal, found across much of North America. They're an intelligent carnivore, related to bears and the giant panda of China. 'Coons live in wooded areas, usually along streams or ponds, and they will eat whatever their environment provides. In undeveloped areas, they dine on fish, frogs, insects, and whatever else they can find. Years ago, my uncle Harold despaired of harvesting sweet corn on his southern Minnesota farm. No matter where he planted sweet corn the raccoons would find it and raid his crop, even in the middle of a field planted to corn for livestock feed.

'Coon hunting is a popular sport in many areas of the country. In the community in eastern North Dakota, where we used to live, I knew one person who kept a pack of hounds and spent many sleepless nights following his pack as they chased raccoons through wooded river bottoms.

The urban raccoon is a thornier problem. They raid garbage cans. They nest and bear young in chimneys. They force their way into attics and crawlspaces of houses. They also raid gardens and fruit trees. In short, they eat whatever their environment provides and the urban and suburban environment is full of food for an enterprising 'coon.

So, what should my daughter do with her masked raiders? I facetiously suggested she get a .22 rifle and set up an ambush. Of course, shooting within city limits is one of those things almost universally forbidden. Oakland has enough problems with firearms violence in inner city neighborhoods without people in the hills shooting raccoons.

Another possibility is to call an animal control agency to trap her raccoons. I suggested she blow their minds by specifying that she doesn't want any of this catching them and releasing them, unharmed, in the hills. They already live in the hills and that's the problem. "Can't you just see their reaction," I suggested, "when you tell them, 'Just knock 'em in the head with a ballpeen hammer, and try not to ruin any of the meat. I don't want them released unharmed. I want them for dinner.'"

Raccoon for dinner? I had roasted raccoon some years ago, after my brother disposed of one on the farm. It had dark meat, like beef or venison, but tasted much like pork. It can also be ground and mixed with venison to make sausage.

Raccoons hold a special place in Native American folklore. The raccoon is the trickster, the sly and crafty animal that may appear slow, but is actually quick and agile; the opponent who outsmarts his enemies and uses his hands like a human.

For a lucky few, barbecued raccoon may also provide a memorable dinner.

I wrote a column about Erin's raccoon problems and even included a recipe I'd picked up on the Internet. I got a lot of comments from my readers, with most people saying, "Thanks, but I'll pass on raccoon." One reader went on to suggest that if she found any dead bobcats in her neighborhood, "please spare us a recipe for sausage lynx."

At the time, Erin worked for a North Carolina company and she passed my column along to co-workers in the home office. Many responded enthusiastically to the prospects of a 'coon cookout. One person wrote, "My grandma used to make a great barbecue 'coon. I haven't had any since I was 10, but she could make it taste like chicken. You brought back good memories."

Another recalled, "I've had 'coon several times at my grandmother's house. It was quite tasty. She served it barbecued, in sausages, and in burgers. She usually served the burgers for breakfast with biscuits and eggs."

"You guys are making me homesick for all the culinary wonders my family used to make when I lived in NC," another southerner commented. "Nothing like squirrel or bunny gravy, or BBQ beef or fried frog legs or…I think I'm going to cry!"

With a note of caution, still another reader suggested cooking raccoon to an internal temperature of 160 - 170 degrees, which drew this plaintive note, "So, do you mean, I'm going to have to put a meat thermometer in this thing…I'm from the city…"

I have a couple cookbooks on the bookshelf next to me. *Wild Game Cookbook*, from the Remington Sportsmen's Library, has recipes for many small game animals, many of which some people might decline, including beaver, rabbit, opossum, woodchuck, muskrat and, of course raccoon. *Savoring the Wild* is a cookbook published by Falcon Press, with favorite recipes from Montana Fish, Wildlife & Parks employees, featuring recipes for squirrel, raccoon, beaver, woodchuck and muskrat. Surprisingly, neither cookbook has recipes for rattlesnake.

On the premise of "If you don't catch any fish, you can at least eat the bait," A. D. Livingstone, who for many years wrote about game and fish cooking in *Gray's Sporting Journal*, once wrote about bait delicacies, including deep-fried "Cricket Crisps," stir fried "Mealworms al dente," and for an appetizer, large grasshoppers, wrapped in thinly sliced bacon, sprinkled with parmesan cheese, paprika, salt and pepper, and cooked on a kebab skewer over an open fire.

On the African island of Mozambique, according to a 2002 article in *Chile Pepper* magazine, a popular delicacy is mapani caterpillars, usually spiced with peri-peri, a regional hot chile pepper. The caterpillars are so popular they are threatened with overharvesting. The author of the article, Stephen Lay, commented, "It's definitely an acquired taste, but for those who indulge it's a wholesome snack of approximately 60 percent protein."

If you shudder at caterpillar, the people of Mozambique would, I suspect, balk at lutefisk, that traditional Scandinavian delicacy of dried cod, reconstituted in lye water. I don't care for lutefisk but have fond memories of my father's favorite Christmas Eve bedtime snack. After the presents were opened and the last of the company sent home, he'd raid the refrigerator for cold lutefisk and wrap it in lefse—a lutefisk burrito, we might call it. Sitting at the kitchen table, eating his fish burrito, fish juices dripping down his pajama shirt, Dad was a happy man.

Meantime, while we take this little international tour of foods, raccoons continue to infest Erin's neighborhood. California's raccoon season runs November through March. In the city, she can't use firearms, but she can legally use a slingshot or bow and arrow.

After getting advice on weapons options from a local police officer, she invited him and his wife for a potential raccoon dinner, suggesting that if raccoon wasn't to their taste, "I can probably find a pretty good wine to wash it down."

Golden Years, Golden Hours

A Change of Seasons

Chapter 30

Hints of Autumn

For those of us with an urge to wander the mountains and prairies, walking behind a bird dog with shotgun at hand (a Seasonal Affective Disorder, some might suggest) the long wait since January, when last year's waterfowl season ended, is about over.

In Montana, the first of the upland bird seasons open on the first day of September, when hunters can pursue sharp-tailed grouse and sage grouse, Hungarian partridge, and our three mountain grouse, the ruffed grouse, blue (dusky) grouse and Franklin (spruce) grouse.

Waterfowl seasons usually open on a weekend at the end of September or beginning of October. Our pheasant seasons usually begin the second Saturday of October. The bottom line to all these opening dates is that from the first day of September to New Year's Day we can indulge our passions for hunting upland birds, and then slowly wean ourselves away from hunting with a few last duck hunts in early January.

I'm happy to be able to be a hunter in the 21st Century.

I've certainly had envy for people who hunted upland birds in the 19th Century, when there was an explosion of prairie chicken populations, as the Midwest prairies first got broken up and planted to wheat. There are lots of stories about those good old days when a sport might take a train to Fargo, North Dakota, and then hire a wagon and team of horses and head out in most any direction and come back, at day's end, with a wagon box full of pinnated grouse, the proper name for prairie chickens.

I also have some envy for people who were able to hunt pheasants in the Midwest during the war years of the 1940s, and just after. Years ago, as an interviewer for the Social Security Administration, I had many conversations about those glory years with people entering their retirement years. They'd tell stories of just walking into a field and shooting a generous limit of pheasants in just minutes, often adding, "And we didn't have to do any dang walking, either."

For the people who experienced those bird bonanzas, everything after that was downhill.

Still, for all intents and purposes, I'm living in the good old days right now, and I've been enjoying these good old days for much of my life.

Over 60 years ago, in the September 14, 1952 issue of the *Montana Standard*, of Butte, Montana, tucked away behind news of the Korean War and the Eisenhower-Stevenson presidential campaigns, the sports pages reported on pennant races in the then eight-team American and National Leagues. A recurring feature in the Sunday sports section was "Spillum's Scratch Pad," a small advertisement from Spillum's, a long-gone sporting goods store in uptown Butte. The ads generally contained a few short paragraphs of outdoor notes from "Brother" Spillum.

On that particular Sunday, "Brother" wrote, "This morning

(Sunday) starts upland bird season. There are a lot of good places open and hunting should be good. The season runs Sunday, Monday and Tuesday. Just three days. But if you work Sunday you still have a couple days."

Presumably, there were other opportunities to go shotgunning, as that three-day season most likely did not include pheasants, not to mention waterfowl hunting. Still it boggles my mind to think of having just a three-day window of opportunity to wander the aspens, brush patches and clearings for ruffed and blue grouse, not to mention those same three days for sage grouse, sharptails and partridge.

If those three days seem like a short season, consider the plight of the many people who had to work on Monday and Tuesday. If they went to church on Sunday morning before heading for the hills, a flat tire on the way meant, most likely, they missed the whole season.

No doubt there are some old-timers with long memories about those short seasons that could tell tales of some great hunts they had in those hectic few days. I had friends back in North Dakota who recalled, with fondness, when, years ago, the state's deer season was just three days long.

They told stories of how every hunter in the state was out at the same time and simultaneously stomping every bit of wildlife cover. It was, reportedly, a hectic time, with deer running everywhere, and bullets flying. "It was so darned much fun," they'd say, with a happy grin.

We play the cards we are dealt and if we had just a three day upland season I'd be out all three of those days, if possible, and thankful for the opportunity.

On the other hand, I wouldn't willingly trade for those good old days. I enjoy being out in early September, when the weather is often more summer-like than not, and the wildlife habitat is still green and lush.

An important part of the experience, however, is returning, again and again, as the season blends into early autumn.

There is nothing like being afield in early autumn when prairie brush patches are a blaze of reds and oranges, or the mountain aspen thickets when the trees overhead are bright yellow, and the ground is carpeted in gold from fallen leaves.

As autumn's gaudy colors fade into shades of brown and tan, and a gray sky carries the threat of snow, the upland bird hunter is often alone. When I see other hunters, they're usually looking for elk or deer, a much more serious enterprise than my seemingly aimless wanderings behind my Labrador retriever.

I look forward to another season of wanderings, and I think it's appropriate that we celebrate the beginning of September with a holiday weekend. The opening of a new hunting season is an occasion to celebrate. With any luck, the fish will be biting, also.

As Miguel DiCervantes, author of *Don Quixote* asked, "Can we ever have too much of a good thing?"

Chapter 31

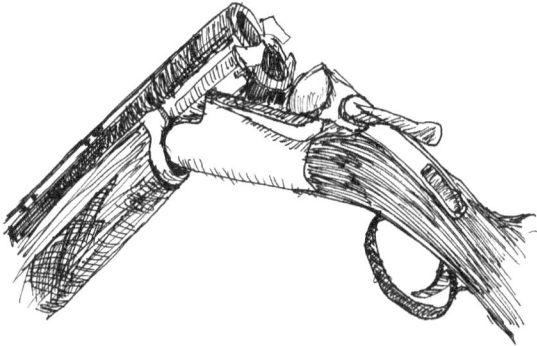

Shotgun Shopping

"Hey, Paul," the voice on the phone said, "It's Steve. I'm shopping for a new shotgun and I need some expert advice."

I paused in tying flies for the Labor Day weekend and said, "I'm not so sure if I'm an expert, but I'll share some of my personal prejudices. What are you looking for?

"I've been using a pump gun for years and I've always been frustrated by how long it takes to refocus for a second shot. I've been thinking in terms of an over/under double barrel, or a semi-automatic. Do you have any thoughts on those guns?"

"Well," I responded, "I've been using an over and under for quite a few years. It's a 20-gauge Ruger Red Label that my wife bought me for an anniversary present in 1992. It's a great gun and has accounted for many limits of pheasants. I like the looks and feel of the over and under. I can't take credit for this, but I remember a gun writer with similar prejudices who considered the semi-automatic shotgun as a 'clanking piece of machinery,' compared to his pet double.

"Of course," I continued, "there are times when I've stood there with an empty gun, when birds are still getting up, or I needed just one more shot to bring down a winged bird. Still, I rarely have reason to regret using a gun that has just two shots before I have to break the gun to reload."

Remembering a frustrating first season with my Ruger, I cautioned, "It may take a little while to get used to the feel and handling of a new gun. I had this tendency to shoot and then try to pump the forearm for the second shot. Of course, by the next year, when I took my old pump out for duck hunting, I couldn't remember to pump for the second shot. I'd stand there pulling the trigger. I solved the problem by getting a 12-gauge over and under for waterfowl."

"You use a 20-gauge for pheasants?" There was disbelief in Steve's voice. "Do you use 3-inch magnum loads?"

"Nope. Just the standard 2-¾ inch one ounce loads of #6 shot. It does the job quite nicely." I added, "I like the 20-gauge. It's a little lighter and easier handling than a 12-gauge gun, with softer recoil. I use it for most of my hunting.

For grouse I usually use a lighter ¾ ounce load of #7 ½ shot."

"Does your gun have a changeable choke? A gun I was looking at had choke tubes ranging from improved cylinder to modified to full choke," indicating the gun would throw a fairly wide to a relatively narrow pattern. "What would you use?"

I suggested using the chokes for a wider pattern, adding, "Personally, I'd order a couple more choke tubes for your gun. The tubes I use in my Ruger are skeet and skeet." Skeet is quite an open choke," I explained. "It's deadly on birds taken at close range and I often surprise myself when I drop pheasants and grouse at long ranges as well. Of course, for that matter, shooting experts have proven that most hunters can't hit anything at ranges of over 30 yards to start with."

"One of the guns I was looking at had a safety that was really stiff and hard to move. In fact I had the salesperson take another one out of the box to see if it was better. It wasn't. Any thoughts on that?"

It didn't take me long to answer that question. "I have a gun in my cabinet like that. It seemed like I scraped my thumb raw every time I shot it. I'd avoid it. In my opinion, you want something that makes gun handling a smooth and easy process. That way, when you're out in the field you can concentrate on the bird when it flushes and not be frustrated by quirks in the gun's mechanics."

I told Steve to enjoy shopping. "It's exciting to shop for a new gun."

"Thanks," Steve said. "This has been a big help. You ought to write a column about this."

"Gee, maybe I will."

I did, and a friend chided me for not suggesting a 28-gauge shotgun. He's primarily a bobwhite quail hunter in a southern Midwest state, and he's a devoted fan of the diminutive 28-gauge shotgun, though he generally uses a semi-automatic gun.

I told him his point was well taken, though I said that Steve was having enough trouble with the concept of using a 20-gauge shotgun for pheasants, without dealing with thoughts of an even smaller load.

There are other shooters who would question why I didn't recommend a 16-gauge gun, the shotgun that, according to its fans, "carries like a 20 and shoots like a 12." The 16-gauge has a lot of devotees as a shotgun that's easy to carry and still shoots a heavy load. Historians will point back to a time when the governing body of skeet shooters decreed that there would be skeet events for 12, 20 and 28 gauge shotguns, but not 16-gauge. That decision took the 16-gauge out of the spotlight. The problem that most shooters have is finding 16-gauge shells, especially if they're out on a hunt somewhere in the "outback."

Over the years, I've had more thoughts on the topic of shotguns, especially shotguns for upland birds.

That pet gun of mine, the Ruger Red Label 20-gauge, is still a favorite gun for upland birds, though as I've gotten older I've decided that it sure gets heavy on a long walk across the prairies. It weighs in at just over 7 pounds and I really don't think an upland gun that will generally shoot relatively light loads needs that much weight.

In fact, when I'm in a sporting goods store that has a good selection of shotguns I'll often kick a few tires, picking up one shotgun after another and I'm usually dismayed at how heavy many of those guns are. A shotgun that weighs in at 8 pounds, for example, might be okay in a duck blind, where you're not doing much walking, but I'd hate to carry it up a mountain or across the prairies.

A few years ago I enjoyed shooting an ultra-light 20-gauge over and under shotgun at an outdoor writers conference shooting day. It weighed in at just six pounds and it felt good and shot well. When I got home from the conference I mentioned it to my wife and (bless her heart) she suggested I should get it.

Over the summer I thought a lot about it and I finally decided I don't really need two 20-gauge O/U guns in my cabinet. What I really wanted was a 28-gauge over/under.

I shopped around, read a lot of reviews, and finally ended up asking a local store to order a 28-gauge version of the Ruger Red Label. I decided on the Ruger because it would have the same feel and handling characteristics of the shotgun I'd already been carrying around for the previous 20 years. It weighs in at six pounds, and you can take my word for it; over the course of a day's hiking and hunting, there's a big difference between a gun that weighs six pounds and a gun that weighs just a pound more.

As for results in the field, I haven't noticed much difference between the 20 and 28. The load I've been using for pheasants is 7/8 ounce, and that's a marginal difference from the 1-ounce 20-gauge load. When I swing the 28-gauge shotgun on a bird and pull the trigger at the right time, the birds seem to fold and drop. In other words, if I do my job, the gun and the shot shell will do theirs. I try not to take low percentage shots, but even so, I'm occasionally pleasantly surprised when I take a second shot at a pheasant that's heading for the next county and see it drop like a wet rock.

I should mention that several years ago, the Sturm, Ruger Company quit making shotguns. Apparently the manufacturing process had gotten too expensive to be profitable. A couple years later, however, Ruger came out with a re-engineered Red Label in the 12-gauge configuration. It has gotten rave reviews from many gun writers. There were hints that the company would come out with 20 and 28-gauge versions at a later date, but as of now (2018) Ruger is out of the shotgun business. Of course, if you wanted to check the used gun market I don't think there'd be any problem finding the lighter guns.

I don't use the 28-gauge for waterfowl. For ducks, and the occasional goose that might blunder within shooting range, I prefer using my 12-gauge over/under. There are just a lot more choices in non-toxic shotgun shells in 12-gauge. On that note, I generally don't buy those super magnum loads for ducks. I've been perfectly happy using 2-¾ inch steel shot loads when I jump-shoot ducks. As I said before, when I do my job, the gun and load will do its job. You don't need to punish yourself with a 3-½ inch magnum load to collect a duck dinner.

I occasionally use my 20-gauge gun for ducks, but I do use a 3-inch magnum load for waterfowl.

I might mention that I love the classic looks of side-by-side double barrel shotguns, and, in fact, with side-by-side doubles there are a lot more guns on the market that are lightweight for the upland hunter. As much as I like them, however, I don't shoot them well. Some people note that American shooters tend to learn shooting with a small caliber rifle and tend to do better with shotguns that have that single barrel sighting plane. I guess I fit that profile.

Some people call 28-gauge shotguns "the old man's upland gun."

That profile fits as well.

For the bottom line, however, I'll note that shooting 28 gauge shotgun shells comes with a financial penalty. You'll rarely find them at a discounted sales price, and before going on a trip you'd better make sure you have a good supply of shells, because you probably won't find them at any price at the local hardware store in your hunting area.

Chapter 32

Grouse Training Camp

It's been a tough fall training camp, up on that western Montana mountain.

Trudging up and down those mountainsides, I couldn't help thinking back to those long ago twice-a-day football practices back in high school. Those sweaty sessions under a steamy August sun were a long time ago, to be sure. In fact, I have to concede that the last time I put on cleats and pads, President Dwight Eisenhower was running for reelection, if that's any indication.

Still, the goal of those practices: to get in good physical condition so that playing football games would seem easy in comparison, seemed altogether too much like the opening of the upland bird season over Labor Day weekend.

In recent years we've spent Labor Day weekends camping at a Forest Service campground convenient to both flyfishing and grouse hunting. There's a road that loops its way to near the top of a mountain and over the years I've established about five different areas that have blue grouse. There are other areas on the mountain that look pretty much the same to me, but I never found grouse there. I guess you'd have to ask the grouse why they never go to these other spots. If you can find them, that is.

On opening day we drove up that mountain road before dawn and halfway up the mountain I spotted a covey of grouse on the road. The birds nervously moved off the road when Flicka, my Labrador retriever hunting partner, and I made our approach, but we managed to get shots at the flushing birds and dropped one of them. With one bird in hand we pounded the bush but the birds had scattered and didn't want to be found.

At the top of the mountain we ran into another covey of grouse. I missed a shot at one bird, but another flew directly at me, about 15 feet off the ground. It's an easy shot to miss, but I got this one. The bird folded, though its momentum carried it so that it actually crashed into and bounced off my leg. Flicka was at my side and caught it in midair on the bounce—an easy retrieve, in fact the easiest retrieve of her entire career.

On another sagebrush ridge we put up just a couple birds that flushed at the edge of shooting range. I got off a couple shots but nothing dropped. We had friends coming to our camp for lunch that day so that ended that first day of hunting. I felt pretty good about getting a couple of those big, chunky birds.

In succeeding mornings, however, those grouse outfoxed Flicka and me at every turn. They'd flush when we were still 50 or so yards away. If we followed them into the timber they'd flush from the tops of trees, and I long ago learned the hard way that that's about as tough a shot as they come.

I called the birds blue grouse, though if you look in the upland hunting regulations you'll see the birds referred to as "dusky" grouse. In 2006, the American Ornithological Union designated blue grouse into two different strains. The grouse of inland mountains are now officially dusky grouse and the grouse of Pacific coastal mountains are "sooty" grouse. Of course, if you're talking to any other hunters, chances are they'll look at you quizzically if you call them dusky grouse instead of blues.

Whatever you call those grouse, don't call them fool hens. While blue grouse, or dusky grouse, if you want to be correct, often have a reputation for innocence, I can take you trekking across a mountain where I know grouse are to be found. But after they've flushed at long distance, or flushed where a big tree screens their escape flight, you may start calling those grouse some new names, but fool hen won't be one of them.

There may be fools on the mountain, but it's the hunters, not the grouse.

"There should be a law against leaving a shotgun in its case all summer. The thing loses all sense of direction and has no more pointing sense than a St. Bernard pup." Burton Spiller from *Drummer in the Woods*.

Burt Spiller was a well-known writer back in the 1940s, best known for stories about New England ruffed grouse hunting, at a time when New England was much more rural—a time of hunting old, abandoned farms grown to brush and aspens, with grouse hanging around forgotten apple orchards, or perching on crumbling stone walls.

The above quotation comes from a now out-of-print book, *Drummer in the Woods*, a collection of stories previously published in magazines such as *Field & Stream*, though one chapter, notably, was first published in *Cosmopolitan* magazine. This goes back when *Cosmo* was more of a general interest magazine than it is now. Somehow, a ruffed grouse story lurking amidst the somewhat more spicy articles of the current *Cosmopolitan* seems unlikely.

Still, that quotation rang all too true while reading the book during the Labor Day weekend following a frustrating morning of chasing blue grouse.

The sun was just lighting up the tops of the mountains when Flicka and I began our first walk of the new hunting season. We walked up and around a hilltop and Flicka picked up bird scent. In seconds a covey of grouse was taking to the air. I got off a couple hurried shots, but to no effect.

An hour later, Flicka put up some more birds and again shots rang out on the mountainside—as the grouse flew off, none the worse for wear.

Fortunately, these birds were slow learners. They settled into an old clear cut farther down the hillside. We put up the birds again and this time I shot a double on the covey rise.

Scoring a double doesn't happen too often—at least the way I shoot. A true double is when you shoot two birds that flush at the same time. If they get up one at a time that doesn't count. A few years back I got a true double on ruffed grouse, actually more difficult, as ruffed grouse tend to hang around in heavier cover. Last season I got lucky with a "Scotch double," when we put up a covey of Hungarian partridge, and a second bird happened to be in the same line of fire as the bird I was swinging on. When two birds fell I was so surprised I forgot about taking another shot at the disappearing birds. That would have been a rare opportunity for a triple on a covey rise—with a gun that holds just two shells.

I got in more shooting that morning, though the sad reality was that I had a dozen empty shotgun hulls rattling around in my hunting vest and just those two grouse to show for it.

If my shooting was less than stellar, it was still an exciting morning, as the big news was that there seemed to be a good grouse population on the mountain. The last time I'd hunted that mountain we saw a total of just two blue grouse in three days of hunting. This time, by the end of the hunting weekend we had put up five separate flocks of grouse.

As for my first love, ruffed grouse, while relaxing outside after a morning of hunting, I spotted a couple ruffed grouse walking in tall grass in our campsite. I finally released Flicka to check them out and she flushed something like nine or ten juvenile birds.

Oh, and the shooting did improve after that first day. A few days later I had successful shots at two blues, with just two shells. As Burt Spiller wrote later in that article, "If the gun couldn't do it alone, I'd have to help it next time."

Chapter 33

Passing of the Torch

One of my favorite thingsis to take a hike in the aspens when the fall colors are at their peak. That period doesn't last long. The colors peak around the end of September or early October. Then fall rains and wind come, overnight the leaves fall and the aspen-colored mountainside is grayish brown, waiting for winter.

Of course, one of the best parts of hiking in the aspens is the search for ruffed grouse. I love hunting for pheasants and other upland birds, but my favorite upland species is the ruffed grouse. I hope I never have to make a choice, but if forced to select just one bird to chase through the autumn months, ruffed grouse would be my personal choice.

Those colorful aspen thickets are a big reason for loving ruffed grouse. To be sure, you might find them in the willows along a creek bottom or sheltering in some conifers during a snowstorm, but if there aren't aspens around you won't find grouse. The aspens provide grouse with a year 'round home, with shade and protection from predators, patches of sunlight where the sun comes through openings in the overhead canopy, varied ground cover that includes clovers and berries. During winter months, grouse switch to an exclusive diet of aspen buds. Aspens are more than a home, they're the grouse's grocery store.

Walking into an aspen stand, especially during fall colors, is like walking into a cathedral, to my way of thinking. It's a place full of color, light, and life.

In late September of 2006, on one of the season's first walks in the aspens, the color and light really struck me, as a few days earlier I'd been on a storm-swept tip of an Alaskan island that was all socked in with rain and fog. The island is densely vegetated, but on that stormy day the colors seemed to be mainly shades of iron and aluminum.

Of course, as I started climbing up some steep draws it occurred to me as I huffed and puffed that spending a week at sea level isn't ideal preparation for trudging up mountainsides over a mile high.

My meditations were interrupted by the sight and sound of a ruffed grouse flushing from near my feet, making for the safety of another stand of aspens on the other side of the little creek that goes through the bottom of the draw. I hurried my first shot and missed but my second shot caught up with the grouse. I didn't see the bird fall, but I could hear it flapping its wings in the trees as it unsuccessfully tried to maintain flight.

I told Flicka, then just over a year old, "Go get it!"

She ran into the brush and immediately came back without anything. "Come on, girl," I said, "find that bird." Again she went in and came back empty-mouthed. "Am I going to have to help you?" I grumbled as I started climbing down the steep creek bank. I had just gotten to the bottom when Flicka emerged from the brush with a wounded, but still alive, ruffed grouse in her mouth.

"Good girl!" I exclaimed. "That's your first ruffed grouse. I'm so proud of you."

It's hard telling, of course, what Flicka thought about all the fuss I was making over her. For most retrievers, the job of retrieving is the ultimate reward of the hunt. What could be better than holding a bird in your mouth as your entire being is flooded with the scent of grouse?

For me, this little scene had a sense of déjà vu, as on the last Friday of September, one year earlier, my old Lab, Candy, and I collaborated for the first ruffed grouse of 2005 from that same clump of brush overlooking that same little creek. Candy had moved on to retirement and was now living with our daughter in California.

On this last Friday of September 2006, Flicka and I succeeded in the first ruffed grouse of 2006, the first of her career.

I prayed that day that we would have many hunts in our future, as indeed there have been, but on this day I felt, in a symbolic way, that the torch had been passed.

Golden Years, Golden Hours

Chapter 34

Milo Goes Hunting

"Milo, it's Paul. I'm going grouse hunting on Saturday. Are you coming?"

There was silence. Finally, I heard a hesitant, "Sure, I'd like nothing better. I've got a problem, though."

"What's that?"

"I don't have a shotgun. I mentioned it to Rick and he told me not to worry about it unless you actually called me."

"That's okay," I told Milo. "I happen to have an extra shotgun or two. I have a nice little 20-gauge side-by-side double barrel shotgun that's easy to carry, and if you behave yourself I'll even let you have some shells, too.

"Gee, that'd be great. Tell you what…I'll have Hazel fix us lunch. What else do I need?"

I hated to have him spend a bunch of money, but some things you've got to have. "Milo, some things you'll need; first, a pair of comfortable boots, because we're going to be doing a lot of walking. Get boots that have a good grip on them, because a smooth-soled boot could slip. Also, anybody hunting with me has to have an orange vest and cap. You'll look like a pumpkin, but there are worse things. One other thing, you do have a hunting license?"

"Yeah, I have a Conservation License, and for us over 62, that's good for both fishing and upland birds."

"Sounds like we're set. I'll swing by early in the morning."

Milo was waiting in front of the house on Saturday morning when I pulled up. We put his lunch cooler and vest in the back of the truck and when he opened the passenger-side door to the truck, Flicka quickly introduced herself. They were old friends by the time we got to the mountains, where a road led us to a grassy hillside and some long sagebrush-covered ridges.

"We'll start here," I told Milo. "People say that blue grouse like to fly down from the pines to feed on grasshoppers early in the morning. Sometimes it even happens that way. We'll let Flicka work ahead of us. If there are grouse out there she'll pick up their scent and flush them for us to shoot at."

We started walking across the mountainside. We were huffing and puffing our way back up one of those ridges when it happened. Flicka began to get excited, as she followed bird scent hanging in the grass. Four grouse got up from a clump of sagebrush. I picked out a bird that was swinging off to the left and pulled the trigger. The bird's flight suddenly stopped, as the load of shot caught up with it. Flicka ran over and brought the big blue grouse to me.

"Wow, that happened so fast I never thought of shooting," Milo said as he came over to see my grouse. "So that's a blue grouse. It looks big, doesn't it?"

"It is a big, chunky bird," I agreed. "Of Montana's woodland grouse, the blue grouse is definitely larger than either the ruffed grouse or Franklin grouse. Let's get some more."

We didn't see any more grouse in the grassy ridges, so we walked into the timber. I called Milo over to look at some little red berries growing along the ground. "Milo, these red berries have several names. They're grouse whortleberry, a variety of lingonberry, but they're commonly called grouse berries. Grouse love to eat them. So be alert, some birds might be hanging around here."

A moment later, a couple grouse flushed off into the trees. Milo flicked off the safety, swung the little shotgun like an old pro, and a big blue came tumbling down.

Flicka brought the bird to me. I handed it over to Milo, who admired the bird for a minute before putting it in the game pouch in the back of his vest. As the bird bounced against Milo's back, I could tell by his grin that you're never too old to enjoy the thrill of a first grouse and the feel of birds in the vest.

After lunch we stopped at a creek to catch some brook trout, so it was late afternoon when I dropped Milo at his house. At the door, he turned and called, "Same time next week?"

Postscript: The week after this story of taking Milo the Miner out for a grouse hunt was published, my friend and editor, Rick Foote, wrote a piece telling that the day after our hunt, Milo came over to my house with the frozen grouse and the sad story that his wife, Hazel, wouldn't let him keep the bird in the house. And, so, Milo's short grouse-hunting career came to an early end.

Golden Years, Golden Hours

Chapter 35

Autumn Mixed Bag

I thought it would be a deal she couldn't refuse.

On a September weekend of camping, fishing and grouse hunting, I suggested to my wife, "Why don't you come along with your mushroom field guide and pick mushrooms while Flicka and I look for grouse?"

After the soaking rains of early September followed by relatively mild and sunny weather there had been an explosion of mushrooms in the mountain woodlands. They're growing on stumps or emerging from decomposing leaf litter in the aspen thickets. I'm pretty sure a lot of them are edible, though a guideline you ignore at your own risk is to never eat a wild mushroom unless you're certain about its identity.

My wife has the advantage here. She studied mycology (the study of fungi) as part of her college biology major and understands the scientific lingo when a guidebook discusses the identifying characteristics of mushrooms.

While I thought it was a great offer, she still passed it up. Go figure.

So I wander the forest, looking at thousands of mushrooms and wonder about them.

On the other hand there are some mushrooms that are not only edible; they're easy to identify. In spring and early summer morel mushrooms are treasures when you can find them.

Puffballs are edible mushrooms that are easy to find and identify. In fact I often have puffballs growing in my yard, though they're usually too small—marble-sized—to make picking worth the effort. Usually when I pick them they're golf ball sized or larger.

On an early October hunt I could hardly believe it when I looked down and spotted a softball-sized puffball. "It's going to be all mushy," I told myself, not wanting to get too excited about my find. I gave it a squeeze and it was nice and firm, just the way a good mushroom should be. I added it to my game bag and continued on my way.

While that softball-sized puffball was a prize it's far from a trophy. I've seen them as large as a basketball and they get bigger than that. The trick is getting a large puffball that's still fit to eat. According to a couple Internet sources, when the puffball flesh is soft or looks yellowish or green, it's no longer edible. In its final phase the puffball flesh dries and if you step on it a puff of powder comes out. Each of those little grains of powder is a spore capable of starting a new puffball. The number of spores in a giant puffball can be trillions. That's a lot.

Perhaps if I left that puffball where it was, next year the whole hillside might have been covered with puffballs. We'll never know because after bringing it home we sliced it and fried it in butter. That mushroom is gone.

While the puffball was a treat, it was just a bonus to the outing. Ruffed grouse were the goal of the trip and when Flicka and I finished our hike up and down the hills we had flushed several grouse and gotten two of them.

After we finished the hunt I drove on to the Big Hole River. After a late lunch in the shade of a golden cottonwood tree I rigged up a flyrod and waded up the river. It was mid-afternoon and the main dry fly action of the day was over. One trout came up and looked at my fly and turned away.

A couple minutes later another trout wasn't so fussy and took the fly. This trout wasn't a bit happy about being fooled into taking an artificial bug but after a few minutes I was able to bring it to hand long enough to unhook it and send it back to get a little bigger, though to tell the truth a 20-inch brown trout is just fine as it is.

We'd had a real western Montana day. A pleasant walk through the aspens on a golden October day, two ruffed grouse, a giant puffball and a nice brown trout.

I love living in Montana.

Golden Years, Golden Hours

Chapter 36

Pheasant U

"I think Flicka is the hero of the hunt."

Looking at Flicka, who was looking, alternately, at Chuck and then me, eyeing, expectantly, our sandwiches, I responded, "Hero? I don't know about that. She's definitely a champion moocher."

But Chuck was right. Flicka was the hero of the hunt, and this was her first real pheasant hunt. Chuck is Chuck Rushing, a retired police officer who lives in Glendive, Montana. We'd gotten acquainted at Kiwanis events, and at an August convention we decided we needed to do more than just talk about getting together for a pheasant hunt.

Flicka is now the veteran of hundreds of hunts since her first puppy hunts in the late fall of 2005, but this particular hunt was on the opening weekend of the 2006 Montana pheasant season.

That previous December, when she was just five months old, she learned the scent of pheasants and the sound of a shotgun. In the weeks before the pheasant opener we'd been hunting ruffed grouse and blue grouse with some success. Still, the opening of pheasant season for this overgrown puppy was kind of like sending a bright middle school student off to university.

The learning began quickly. A pheasant flushed from the base of a cut bank of an old gravel pit. Before the pheasant disappeared over the top I managed to swing my gun and shoot. I saw the bird fold as it disappeared from sight. "Go get it, Flicka," I said, gesturing for her to run up and fetch the bird. She ran up to the top of the bank and looked back, as if to ask, "Now what?"

She disappeared and then came back a moment later with my pheasant in her mouth. "Is this what you wanted?" her body language seemed to say. "Good girl, Flicka," I told her, "bring it here." She delivered the pheasant, a long-tailed yearling rooster; her first pheasant retrieve.

While the hunting was never easy, over the next three days she matured as a pheasant dog. With the scent of pheasant firmly locked into her memory, she repeatedly found pheasants hiding in thick weed patches and brush jungles. Sometimes she picked up the scent too well. With a strong wind blowing across a stubble field, several times she took off at a dead run. I tried to bring her back but the scent was too strong. Her chase ended with a bird taking to the air a hundred yards off.

While she had some miscues, she made up for it by picking up scents in heavy cover, tracking zigzag courses through tall weeds and grasses until she put up a pheasant. All too often the bird was a protected hen, but sometimes a cock pheasant was the end of the chase, and if we did our job, the bird ended up in the back of our hunting vests for a one way trip to be guest of honor at a pheasant dinner.

A precious memory from that first morning of our pheasant hunt is when I decided it was time for a break, and I sat down on a grassy hillside and got a candy bar from my vest. Flicka sat down beside me and leaned against me, a tangible communication of love. I could almost hear those gears in her brain clicking and sending this message, "Thanks! This is the most fun I've ever had."

Flicka comes from a pointing Lab background and by the second day of hunting that pointing instinct was coming through as she'd often pause before pouncing on a clump of weeds sheltering a tight-holding pheasant. Along the edge of a creek, she locked up on a tight-holding bird. It's almost like she was daring the bird to fly. When she couldn't stand it any longer, she backed up a bit and then, from a different angle, pounced, and up came the rooster. It's a quick, quartering away right-to-left shot, but the bird dropped like a stone and Flicka made a retrieve.

Another pheasant headed for safety in the trees on the other side of the creek. I missed with my first shot but dropped the bird with the second and the pheasant dropped into tall grass on the bank. This would be Flicka's first water retrieve, but she did it like a pro, swimming across to get it and bringing it back and up the bank to deliver it to me.

The last pheasant of the weekend came at the end of a stroll through a weed patch heavy with frost. Flicka was soaking wet from melting frost but paid no attention as she patiently followed a scent trail through the cover. When we reached the edge of the weeds the air was full of pheasants. Most of the birds were hens, but I spotted a rooster taking off. I got off a shot that scratched the bird down. The bird hit the ground running but Flicka was on it immediately. A couple times I saw the bird jump in the air as if trying to fly, but this was a race that Flicka was destined to win.

Was there a bit of swagger in her stride as she brought that bird back? If so, it was well earned. She had graduated from Pheasant U.

Flicka's education from that confused puppy of a year ago to a pheasant dog involved more than a few bumps in the road, but I wouldn't have missed graduation day for anything.

Golden Years, Golden Hours

Chapter 37

Perfection Happens

Flicka went into the aspens searching for bird scent and a few minutes later went on point. I had to climb up a steep bank at the bottom of the hillside to get behind her, and a moment later, Flicka couldn't stand it any longer. She lunged at the cone of scent and with a rush of wings the ruffed grouse took to the air.

I took a quick shot at the bird and missed, following with another shot, missing again. As the bird disappeared off into the forest I stood there pulling the trigger of my now empty gun, wishing that the shotgun was a repeater instead of a double barrel, and that I had one more chance at the grouse.

Though I could see I missed, Flicka went off to retrieve the bird. She reluctantly came back after I blew my whistle for her to return. Bless her little Labrador retriever heart, she had confidence in my shooting, even when I knew that my shots missed the mark.

Flicka wanted to get back out in search of the downed bird. "You shot the gun," her body language seemed to say. "There must be a bird out there, right?" All I could do was apologize.

A little over a week earlier, we were hunting pheasants in North Dakota. Flicka and I were hunting alone that day. The skies were clear with a chilly wind, though a few minutes of walking warmed us up.

The lakeside cover is tough going, with tall weeds and brush. It would be a lot easier to walk in the prairie grasses a little higher up, but pheasants like the nasty cover, so that's where we hunt. Suddenly a cock pheasant flushed. I swung on the bird and pulled the trigger. The bird went down and Flicka quickly found it and brought it to me. I took time to smooth the feathers of the bird and admired its bright plumage before putting it in the back of my vest.

We continue our walk, meandering through the brush, tall grasses and other cover. On a hillside where the edge of the Wildlife Management Area borders croplands, we put up a number of hen pheasants plus a couple birds just out of range that might have been roosters. Sometimes it's hard to pick out those colors when the light is wrong.

Our ramble across the prairie next went to a thin line of trees. A few years ago a fire had swept across part of the area. After a couple wet years there's little sign of that fire except for that line of blackened dead trees. Flicka locks up on point and when the pheasant flushes I get an easy shot and Flicka gets an easy retrieve.

Just a couple minutes later Flicka again goes on point next to a clump of brush, a tangle of weeds, tall grass, and fallen tree limbs. When she finally breaks point a cock pheasant takes to the air. While the bird's flight takes twists and turns through the trees, I stay focused on the bird and when I pull the trigger the bird folds, and Flicka makes the retrieve.

Then it occurs to me that we've collected a three-bird limit of pheasants with just three shots. It had been something like 55 years since I first ventured out into a field with a shotgun in search of pheasants. In terms of shooting success it has been a long progression since those early years when dropping any flying bird seemed akin to a miracle. Actually, it's not that long a progression since early September when I went through 12 shells to produce two blue grouse on the season's first day of hunting.

Over the years, especially the last few decades when one of several Labrador retrievers have been my partner, I've gotten limits of pheasants many times, but this was the first time I've limited out with firing just three shells.

Wingshooting involves luck, experience, good dog work, shooting skills, and above all, focus. As we remind ourselves in tennis, "Keep your eye on the ball."

Still I wondered if I'd ever again summarize a day's hunt as "Three birds up. Three shots. Three retrieves."

Flicka and I went hunting the next day and we came close to another perfect hunt.

We were walking through an old alfalfa field in another part of the Wildlife Management Area we'd hunted the previous day. The cover was twisted and tangled, reminding me of some of the fields we walked back at the end of the old Soil Bank days in the early 1960s.

We were just ten minutes into our walk when Flicka flushed a rooster pheasant. It's kind of a tough shot and I miss with my first shot, but I connect with the top barrel and scratch the bird down. The bird lands running and takes Flicka on a merry chase, but she catches up with the rooster and brings the bird back to me.

We walked down the hill to the edge of the lake where several pheasants flushed wild. We work the shoreline cover and Flicka locks up on point. When the bird comes up it's a rooster and I drop it with my first shot, with the bird landing with a big splash in shallow water in the bay.

We don't go much farther when Flicka again goes on point and puts up another rooster, which I drop on my first shot, and Flicka retrieves the long-tailed bird, which had 24-inch tail feathers.

We've got another limit of pheasants, and again we had three pheasants up and three retrieves, though today it took four shotgun shells.

Perfection is, of course, an elusive goal. I play French horn in a community symphony orchestra and a continuing goal is to play a concert without making any mistakes. I've come close and I can usually say in all honesty that I gave it my all. Still, the pursuit of perfection will usually bring more frustration than rewards.

For a number of years a weekly outing through the summers was to go trap shooting at a gun club near our town. I often saw new shooters come in that had natural hand and eye coordination and they'd start hitting 25 straight targets after just a few tries, or as some veteran shooters would say, "I straightened that one out." Eventually, I straightened out a few rounds, though not often enough to ever think I should get serious about trap shooting.

Trap shooting is good preparation for upland bird hunting. Skeet and sporting clays might be better practice, though any of the shooting games will improve gun handling and shooting skills. If I have some hunts when almost everything seems to go well it's a direct result of those thousands of clay pigeons I shot at.

So, would I ever achieve perfection again?

A couple years after this hunt, on our annual trip to the Rocky Mountain Front of Montana, I started a hunt on Bill's ranch, walking across a hillside just below an irrigation canal that cuts across the property. This was a year with a lot of winter snow, followed by heavy spring and summer rains. The vegetation, grass, weeds, is higher than I'd ever seen it here.

The last couple years on this ranch I was disappointed by the small numbers of pheasants, so I wondered if the abundant cover might hold more birds.

Just a few minutes into our walk, Flicka went on point and then put up a rooster pheasant from a clump of willows. I swung on the bird and I can see that I hit it, just before it disappeared from sight. When the pheasant flushed, a couple Huns also flushed and a white-tail deer popped out of the brush.

Flicka picked up the pheasant's scent and she followed it across a shallow draw at the edge of the willows where she went on point before diving into the grass and coming up with the bird.

About then, Bill drove up on the two-track trail on the edge of the irrigation canal and we had a friendly chat about weather, weeds, this year's pheasant population, etc. We finally finished solving these and other problems of the world. Bill drove back to his house to do some chores and Flicka and I resumed our walk.

We worked our way to a patch of willows and Russian olives that's often been a hot spot. Several pheasants flushed as we come down the hill and I got a shot at a rooster crossing from right to left. The bird folded. Flicka ran to retrieve the pheasant when another bird flushed, giving me a left to right crossing shot. I make this shot, too.

Flicka dropped the bird she was retrieving and ran to get the new pheasant. She forgot all about the bird she was carrying first, but I had no trouble picking it up.

This was an amazing hunt. We had our day's limit of three pheasants in just half an hour, and that includes ten minutes of shooting the bull with Bill. Then it struck me that I got these three pheasants with just three shots. Maybe the dog work was a little unorthodox, with Flicka dropping one bird to find another, but still, I've just had another perfect hunt, from the standpoint of not missing shots.

We had a leisurely walk back to the truck with my vest heavy with a limit of well-fed pheasants. We took a lunch break and then did another walk to see if we could find some more Huns to add to the bag, but they eluded us. It doesn't dampen our spirits, as we're back in camp and have a leisurely afternoon for cleaning birds and taking a hot shower before we settle in for the evening.

It's two years later, and we're again on our annual outing to the Rocky Mountain Front.

We're starting the first of three days of hunting, camping at a popular Wildlife Management Area. Before going to the farm I have lined up for the day, I stop to gas up in town and have a conversation across the pumps with a frustrated hunter. He's taken the whole week off for hunting and as of Wednesday morning he hasn't fired a shot, and in fact has seen only two pheasants.

The weather forecast was for a 30 percent chance of rain for today. It isn't raining when we gear up for our first walk, but the cold wind suggests that a windbreaker might be a good idea.

This farm isn't large by western standards. In fact, it's downright small. The magic part of the farm is a grassy hillside on the south side of the property and bisecting the hillside is a boggy draw with springs that drain into a tiny creek. Along the draw are patches of willows and cattails. The property line is at the top of the hill and typically, when we walk the draw, I often see flocks of pheasants flushing far ahead and flying over the hill where they're off limits.

This time, however, a couple other hunters are driving along the top of the hill on the other side of the fence line, and watching my progress. We don't see any pheasants.

We circle away from the draw and I'm walking along the top of an irrigation ditch. Flicka is working some cover in the bottom of the ditch when a cock pheasant flushes from right beside me. I shoot and drop the bird on the other side of the ditch. Flicka is going crazy trying to find the bird, though she can't quite get the idea that she needs to go over the top of the ditch bank. I finally work my way down the steep bank and up the next one and gesture to Flicka that this is where she needs to go. She goes just six feet and finds the pheasant, stone dead.

We circle back down the boggy draw and several pheasants flush out of range before Flicka goes on point and two birds flush, a hen and a rooster. I drop the rooster on a left to right crossing shot.

With two birds in the back of the vest, and feeling rather chilled from the wind and a light drizzle that started during our walk, it's time to walk back to the farmstead for a sandwich and a chance to warm up.

After lunch we work a barley stubble field and we put up a number of pheasant hens along an irrigation ditch, but the only rooster we see flushes wild, out of range.

We walk back up to the hillside and, again in the boggy draw, Flicka goes on point and puts up a rooster, giving me an easy shot and Flicka an easy retrieve.

We have our limit of pheasants for the day and have done it with just three shots; another perfect hunt.

On the way back to camp, I stop at the convenience store where I'd gotten gas that morning to pick up a newspaper. The store clerk figures me for a hunter and asks how I did. "Got my limit," I reply.

"Twelve gauge automatic, full choke?" he asks.

"Nope, 28 gauge, over and under, skeet and skeet."

He shakes his head in wonderment as he rings up the sale.

"You'd better make that last shell count," I told myself, pulling my last shell out of my vest and putting it in the chamber of my shotgun, making sure that the barrel selector of my over/under shotgun was set to the same barrel where I chambered that last, lonely shotgun shell.

This was the third day of my annual pheasant hunt on the Rocky Mountain Front country of northern Montana. When I started hunting two days earlier, I opened up a box of shotgun shells. This box was a leftover from last year. I'd shot five shells from that box, so I started three days of hunting with the 20 shells left in the box.

On my first day of hunting, pheasants were acting scarce at the farm I hunted. Flicka put up a couple birds out of range, and by the time I called it a day I'd had shots at just two pheasants, missing both. I felt bad about getting skunked. This is a farm I've hunted for many years and I've gotten many limits of pheasants there.

Not getting any pheasants wasn't the end of the world, however. At this farm, one of the requirements is to stop at the house for tea, cookies, and conversation. As always, it was a good way to end a hunt, and I drove away feeling fortunate to have such good friends who not only let me hunt but insist that I come back later in the season.

On the second day of hunting I collected a three-bird limit of pheasants, though I missed shots at a couple more birds.

On the morning of my third day of pheasant hunting, I again missed a couple birds before connecting with two rooster pheasants in just five minutes.

I had to reflect on having pleasant weather for mid-October. While it was uncomfortably warm the first day, these following days were just about perfect. It was a bit on the cool side, but not cold, and it was breezy, though not up to the standards of the often-legendary winds of the Rocky Mountain Front.

After taking a break for a sandwich and a chance to rest my tired legs (and Flicka's, for that matter) I took inventory before starting our afternoon walk. From that initial partial box of 20 shells, I now had five shells left. Do I crack open another box of shells to make sure I'd have enough for one more pheasant?

I usually keep in mind the advice of one of my old trapshooting buddies back in North Dakota, "Always bring plenty of bullets," he'd say. I figured I shouldn't have any trouble getting one pheasant with five shells. I was shooting fairly well, after all.

Within just a few minutes into our walk, Flicka went on point at the edge of a weedpatch. When the pheasant flushed I couldn't make out any colors, so thought it was a hen—until I heard the bird scold. It was a rooster, after all. I apologized to Flicka for passing up the shot.

I passed up another shot when Flicka put up a pheasant out of range. Then, working a strip of tall grasses, Flicka put up a rooster pheasant. I rushed my first shot and missed, and missed on the follow-up shot. That left three shells.

A little later, Flicka put up another pheasant along the top of an irrigation ditch. I again shot twice and missed on both barrels. I had one lonely, little shell left.

Within a minute of resuming our walk, Flicka put up another rooster pheasant. I swung on the bird and pulled the trigger. The bird dropped to the ground with barely a wiggle, and Flicka had an easy retrieve.

It was a long, but satisfying, walk back to the truck. I'd managed to collect my day's limit of pheasants, and finished the job with my last shell. Not only that, it was my birthday, double reasons to celebrate.

If we always judge the quality of a hunt by the game we bring home, we're putting too much emphasis on just one of the many complicated reasons we hunt.

Hunting is about more than bringing home critters for the pot, even if the one of the cornerstones of hunting is about putting food on the table. The last few years, Montana has had a hunting season for wolves. There is no closed season on coyotes, and some people get a charge out of shooting prairie dogs and gophers. My bottom line is I don't hunt what I don't plan to eat, and I have no plans to dine on roast wolf, coyote, or prairie dog.

Over the course of a hunting season there are usually many outings that don't result in food on the table. Sometimes we don't see any game. Sometimes we see game but don't get a shot. Sometimes we see game, get some shooting, and still don't get anything. If we love hunting, it's a love that would never survive if we depended on a positive balance sheet.

Just a few weeks after that last "perfect" pheasant hunt I got away for an afternoon hunt for ruffed grouse. I needed the outing. My wife had surgery earlier in the week and, while the procedure went well, after days of running back and forth to the hospital and then being go-fer and nursemaid I was beginning to fray around the edges. Flicka and I needed some time in the aspens.

It's a chilly and breezy afternoon with a few snowflakes in the air, but for November, not a bad day.

Our hunting spot is at the base of a mountain in a Wildlife Management Area. The access road to the area cuts through the middle of the low level aspen and brush thickets, and most hunters use this road to go higher up the mountain in search of elk. My usual way to work this covert is to make a circle of the area on the west side of the road and then cross the road and make a circle of the east side.

We walked into the trees, working our way up a side hill and Flicka got a little too far ahead and flushed a grouse. It's a long shot but I shoot anyway and miss. A few minutes later another grouse flushes but I don't have a shot at it before it vanishes in the trees.

We finished our first circle and crossed over to the east side of the covert, where we work our way down and across a hillside and cross a tiny creek and then up and over a wooded knoll on the other side. At the far edge of the thicket, Flicka flushes another grouse. I'm not ready for the bird and I fumble with the safety for a couple seconds before getting off a shot at the bird—and miss.

We move on to the next thicket and just at the edge of an old logging road a grouse flushes from just a couple feet away. I get a couple shots off at it and miss with both of them, as I watch the grouse fly into pine trees a couple hundred yards up the mountain.

After working the trees for a while we eventually circle back to one of the earlier thickets and at the lower edge of the aspens a grouse flushes, and again I fire both barrels in its direction and again I miss.

This grouse covert is usually good for about a three-hour hunt and it's after 4 p.m. when we emerge from the aspens and trudge back to where I'd parked the truck a few hours earlier.

If I've kept track correctly, in this afternoon walk we put up five ruffed grouse. I had shots at four of them and missed all my shots. I briefly consider that I might be getting too old for ruffed grouse hunting—my reflexes aren't fast enough anymore.

I dismiss this kind of defeatist thinking, however. On the drive home I reflect back on the afternoon's hunt. We'd put up grouse and had some shooting. While I didn't bring home a future dinner or two, I'd gotten out of the house and refreshed my spirits and exercised Flicka, and assured myself that ruffed grouse were thriving in this covert. Best of all, my wife was on the mend after her surgery.

A perfect hunt.

Chapter 38

Life Goes On

A couple days before the big game hunting season started, Flicka and I headed for the mountains for a peaceful afternoon of ruffed grouse hunting before big game hunters took over the landscape.

A few weeks earlier, we walked the aspens while they were glowing with autumn colors, with leaves cascading through the air every time a gust of wind came up, turning the ground into a carpet of yellow and gold.

A week after that, the forest had six inches of new snow and walking turned into a laborious trudge across the suddenly wintry landscape. Some aspen trees still had their fall foliage, looking like one of those special color effects in an artsy black and white movie.

On this day, the landscape had again changed color. Except for occasional tints of color on the few trees that still held some leaves, the mountains were mostly browns and tans, with patches of green from pine trees not yet killed off by pine bark beetles. After a couple snows the aspen leaves that carpeted the forest floor with color a few weeks ago were now brown and already decaying into the soil.

A good reason for escaping for a few hours of grouse hunting was to get away from politics, whether in the form of increasingly negative campaign commercials, news coverage, opinion polls, and all the din and nonsense of a political year. As hunting seasons take place in the fall, it's an inescapable fact of life that every other hunting season comes during yet another political season, with all the trappings that come with politics.

In the mountains, on this sunny, late autumn afternoon, there is peace, quiet, and a sense of serenity.

We're now halfway through the hunting season and before the season finally ends in January, we'll be in winter and mild, sunny afternoons of autumn will be a pleasant memory. On the other hand, a week after this hunt we finally arrived at the end of the political season, with most of the votes counted and winners declared. Depending on the election cycle, we could have a new president and the rest of the political pecking order, from the nation's capitol to local courthouses and city halls, will be pretty well sorted out. No doubt some fear the sky is falling while others are celebrating.

In any event, now that the political season has ended, we can get back to the basics. Stock markets go up and stock markets go down. Politicians win elections and politicians lose elections. We'll take a day to celebrate or mourn over our favorite candidates and then life goes on.

This doesn't mean that I'm not interested in politics. In fact, I'm kind of a politics and news junky. I have strong feelings about a lot of political issues and candidates. On the other hand, during a long career as a Federal employee and manager I walked a careful line to avoid violating Hatch Act prohibitions against partisan politics among Federal employees. It was rather liberating, after I retired from government service, to be able to volunteer in some political campaigns.

Still, campaign seasons come and go. Candidates win and candidates lose. If it seems, occasionally, that my fellow voters don't have the sense to come in out of the rain, I'm pretty sure that in the next election that some of them will come around. Political pendulums swing both ways.

Life goes on, just as after Flicka and I finished sharing a sandwich at the top of a long aspen draw, the hunt went on. In a boggy bottom, with aspens on either side of the draw, Flicka picked up the scent of grouse. The bird, or birds, took a wandering stroll through the woods, picking a berry here and there; mixing in some green leaves it found at the edge of the boggy area. How a dog can pick up a scent and follow it, unraveling the circuitous route the bird took, is one of those mysteries that boggle a hunter's mind. No doubt most dogs would, however, look at us with scorn and tell us it's as obvious as that wart at the end of our nose.

This time, the bird's wandering scent trail ended in a tangle of brush in the middle of the bog, as the grouse took wing and disappeared into the trees, leaving me with just a tantalizing, momentary glimpse.

Grouse coverts are often magical places and the unique magic of this particular mountainside is at the bottom of the hill where springs nourish a bed of watercress before the spring's waters join the small stream farther down the hillside.

In a changing autumn landscape, that spring is a constant, with a steady flow of crystal clear water and the Kelly green of watercress that contrasts with the color of all seasons. It's also the source of an annual watercress salad, a hunting season bonus on which, unlike grouse, we can depend.

The political season was finally over—for a little while. It's time to get back to hunting.

Chapter 39

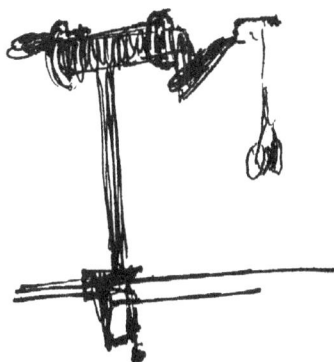

The River in November

Summer was gone. Tourists were safely back in California and other exotic places, their Montana fly-fishing vacation just a fond memory.

It was mid-November. A few days earlier there was snow on the ground and morning temperatures were in the single-digits. Then we had a return to mild weather. The snow melted and I could feel the Big Hole River calling on this hazy Sunday afternoon.

I hadn't been fishing since September, when the weather was still warm, with just a hint of fall in the air. The water was warm enough for wet wading and fish were coming up to 'hoppers. Since then, the lure of the aspens, prairies and marshes have had the upper hand. Fishing could wait.

Now, with winter at hand and several warnings behind us, I decided I needed at least one more day on the river.

It feels strange to return to summer haunts in mid-November. In summer, the river bottoms are green and lush. Songbirds fill the air with their calls and the mosquitoes also insist on attention. In November, the leaves are gone, already decomposing back into the earth, and the dominant color of the bottomlands is brown. The hazy, slanted rays of the sun provide little warmth and the only sounds are from distant waterfowl and the muted whisper of the river.

The high, muddy flows of spring are a distant memory. The water is low and crystal clear, and many sandbars and rocks that sheltered fish from the high waters are high and dry. One run that produced six trout in one day last May was now 30 feet from the water.

The water is icy cold. Even with heavy, wool socks inside my waders I have no urge to do a lot of wading. Casting from the edge of the water seems more tolerable.

Yet, the fish are there. Unlike the birds that nested and raised their young in the river bottoms, they don't have the option of going south with the first blast of cold weather.

In one riffle, where a tree that floated downstream last spring had lodged in the shallows, I'm thrilled at the sudden tug of a fish that has taken my fly. It's not big, but it's good to feel a fish at the end of my fly line and see a bend in my rod. A minute later I've released a 10-inch brown trout back to the river, and regardless of what else happens, I figure the afternoon is complete.

I move upstream to the next pool and I hook another fish that feels bigger. It pulls with authority and even takes out some line. I'm disappointed when the line suddenly goes slack. The fish slipped the hook and returned to the depths without sharing any more secrets.

I found a place to cross the river. The water in the riffle was just knee deep, though as late as August it was too deep and fast to wade. The afternoon is fading, but there's a hatch of tiny insets and I see a couple rises. One more fish takes my fly and fights with strength and determination. In a few minutes I have a 16-inch rainbow at my feet.

The sun was setting as I released that last trout. Trudging back to my parking spot I'm intrigued to see large deer tracks in my footprints of a few hours earlier, where I went through a muddy spot in the brush.

It seemed like ages since last winter and the first fishing outing of the year, when I cast from thick shelf ice at the edge of the Big Hole River to this late autumn afternoon. Hundreds of days, along with millions of gallons of water, have gone downstream, never to be seen again.

As I drove home in the early evening darkness, I felt content. I knew winter would return. For a few hours, however, the river gave me a glimpse of a season and an inner peace that the tourists of mid-summer will never know.

Golden Years, Golden Hours

Chapter 40

Tailfeathers

During the hunting season many hunters head for the hills with the optimistic hope of an opportunity to collect a trophy animal, whether it's a deer, elk, bighorn sheep, or other such critter. Elements such as size of antlers, numbers of antler tines, length and mass of horns, etc., all go into the hunter's judgment of whether we're looking at a trophy-class specimen.

These judgments are often hasty, though I recall a conversation with a couple sheep hunters peering through spotting scopes, leisurely studying bighorn rams on a distant mountainside. "Yeah, that one is probably a 165, if you want to settle for a little one like that," one of the guys commented.

Size is relative of course. Most hunters, who have first beaten the odds to draw a Montana sheep tag, would be thrilled with a ram that scored a 165. It wouldn't quite make the *Boone & Crockett Records of North American Big Game*, or, as many call it, "The Book." To make The Book, your sheep would have to score 180 or better.

Pheasant hunters rarely have that opportunity to study the herd for trophies. The pheasant flushes, often when you're unprepared to shoot, and you're lucky to have time to pick up the bird's colors to decide whether it's a legal rooster or not. Only after you've gotten off a successful shot and retrieved the bird do you have the chance to see if you have a trophy in your hands, and then hope that the bird is still suitable for mounting after getting swatted with a load of lead pellets and then slimed with dog spit in the retrieve.

The pheasant's center tailfeathers are what determine whether a pheasant is a trophy. A month ago, when hunting pheasants in North Dakota with my son, Kevin, we shot several pheasants that seemed to have exceptionally long tailfeathers. When we got home we measured them and the longest came out to 24 inches.

Those feathers came from large, brightly colored cock pheasants that had beaten the odds and survived their first year of life and passed their genes to another generation of pheasants. Run of the mill young-of-the-year roosters usually have tailfeathers of around 15 to 18 inches.

There are many varieties of pheasants, and the birds we see when hunting in North America are generally Chinese ring-necked pheasant. For exceptionally long tailfeathers, however, we need to look at some of the more exotic pheasants, such as the Reeves or Lady Amherst pheasants. These pheasants have 55 to 60 inch tailfeathers, and those long feathers are often used for headdresses such as those used by members of the *Ballet Folklorico de Mexico* in their Aztec dance routine when they put on a show in our city's Community Concert series a few years back.

The longest known tailfeathers in the bird kingdom, according to an Internet search, came from the Crested Argus Pheasant, with a length of 5.7 feet. All these various pheasants originally came from Asia, and according to a British organization, the World Pheasant Association, peacocks and all our domestic chickens are parts of the greater pheasant family of birds.

Exceptionally long feathers, such as those from Amherst and Reeves pheasants, most likely come from pen-raised birds that don't wear down their tail sections walking through weeds, briar patches, and escaping from predators. Indeed, five-foot tailfeathers would seriously endanger a wild pheasant when trying to escape from predators—or a Labrador retriever.

On a gray Sunday afternoon in November 1972, my first Lab, Sam, and I were hunting a ranch along the Tongue River south of Miles City. Sam flushed a pheasant and I made a lucky shot before it disappeared on the other side of some willow trees. We had difficulty finding it, but when we did, the bird's tailfeathers seemed impossibly long, and, when we got home, we measured those center feathers out to a full 26 inches.

A lot of years have come and gone since then and after hundreds of pheasant hunts I have yet to collect a rooster with longer feathers. The closest was one I got in the middle of a Rocky Mountain Front snowstorm about 15 years ago and which tapered to 25 inches.

Those 26-inch tailfeathers of my personal-best pheasant aren't a record as I've read, over the years, of pheasants with 28 and 30-inch tailfeathers.

Still, as I told Kevin, when we admired these long-tailed cock birds at the end of the day's hunt, "If you ever get a pheasant with tailfeathers that are 26 inches or more, you'd better have it mounted, because, believe me, you've got a real trophy."

I could have added that back in 1972 a future pheasant dinner seemed more important than what a taxidermist would have charged for mounting that bird. I've long regretted that decision as the cost would have been long forgotten, but I still remember that on the table, that old pheasant was tough as shoe leather.

Golden Years, Golden Hours

Chapter 41

Orion the Hunter

I climbed to the top of a haystack that overlooks a creek bottom. Settling in for a wait I looked down in the brush and saw a deer looking straight at me. It appeared to be a small white-tailed deer, and a closer look through binoculars confirmed that it had no antlers. We studied each other for a while before the deer decided I was harmless and went back to browsing on some tender twigs.

As the sun went down I could hear a pheasant warm up his rusty vocal cords to announce his presence in that same patch of brush. Where was he a couple hours earlier when by black Lab and I walked through the creek bottom looking for him and his brother?

There's something special about an autumn sunset. As we approach the winter Solstice, the days are short and the sun sets early. The sky is colored by varying hues of orange and purple, while black clouds hang over the western mountains with a vague promise of more seasonable weather.

Suddenly it's dark.

I'm reminded of other days, back in June and July, when the sun doesn't set until after children should be in bed. My Norwegian forebears lived in the far north where the midnight sun and the white nights of summer are a cherished season, making up for the gloom of winter.

I also love those long summer evenings. They're perfect for taking a walk along a quiet country road, looking for deer in their red summer coats to emerge from the lush foliage of mid-summer. My usual preference is to go back to the river, hoping there's an insect hatch that will get the trout feeding before it's too dark to see anything. Then there's the walk back to camp, with bats flitting about in the dark, picking off insects they find with their unique sonar guidance system.

While summer is pleasant, the crisp evenings of fall appeal to my senses. After dark, I look for the constellation Orion, which dominates the southern sky during late fall and winter. I feel an affinity with people of antiquity who didn't have the distractions of artificial lighting and television, but knew their nighttime skies like the backs of their own hands and created imaginative names and stories about the stars.

It's not just Orion; it's Orion the Hunter.

I feel sorry for people who live such urbanized lives they don't recognize constellations in the nighttime skies. Indeed, in cities the night sky is rarely seen because the never-dimming lights of commerce blot out the stars. Even in rural areas of the West it's difficult to get completely away from the electric lights that distract from the beauty of the sky. Mercury vapor lights may make rural living safer, but I miss the days of my youth when all the farms had yard lights, but we only turned them on when we had company.

Looking at Orion in the autumn sky reminds me that I'm a hunter even if I am a poor predator. There is a difference. While sitting under a cottonwood tree a few weeks ago, waiting for a deer, I noted scattered bits of fur, marking where a more efficient predator than I dined on a cottontail rabbit.

While I'm an inefficient predator, I am thankful I live in a part of the world where it is possible to realize one's heritage as a hunter and where being a hunter is an honorable calling. Whether my hunting tool is a shotgun or rifle, or even a fishing rod, I'm thankful that I am able to be part of an ancient tradition, and that I have children and grandchildren who understand that food on the table is not an industrial product.

We live in changing times and not all of us are suited for change. We dispute the management of our natural resources. We disagree about how we should build for the future. We disagree about how we should manage our wildlife.

As change swirls about I try to keep some constants in life. I plan to return to that creek bottom and hope I'll have a chance to stock the freezer for the winter nights to come. Whether I succeed isn't that important. If the sky is clear tonight I'll go out and look for Orion the Hunter and be thankful for these seasons in the outdoors.

Golden Years, Golden Hours

Chapter 42

Winter Can Be Cruel

It's a cruel world, especially in winter.

Late summer and autumn are times of plenty. We harvest gardens and fields. We hunt for elk, deer, and game birds, and put meat in the freezer for the winter months. The fall harvest is, truly, reaping the fat of the land.

And then it's winter, the funnel through which wildlife must go before the renewal of spring. Food is scarce. Spillage from fall harvests has been picked up in the fall months, or been plowed under, or covered with snow. Wild animals are well equipped to forage for food though with colder temperatures they have to spend much more time eating to take on enough calories to maintain body temperature.

Some animals don't make it. Death is a fact of life. Of course, nothing in nature goes to waste. A winterkilled deer or pheasant will feed magpies, ravens, and coyotes, just for a start. When bears emerge from hibernation in spring their first job is to roam the mountainsides in search of winterkills for that first big helping of protein after the long winter's fast.

If winter is a time of hardship it can also be a rude introduction.

A few years ago, just before Christmas, I went to an area ranch for a pheasant outing. The temperatures were hovering at just a degree or so above zero, though after a week of sub-zero weather, it didn't feel too bad. The sun was shining and there wasn't much wind. Flicka, my black Lab, and I dropped into a creek bottom, which had even more shelter from the elements.

We saw pheasant tracks in the snow, though tracks don't always translate to flushing birds. Some pheasants did get up far ahead of us. On this particular day the pheasants weren't waiting around long enough for Flicka to go on point.

We finished a circle in the creek bottom, and were heading to the truck for a lunch break when we came on a pitiful sight.

Along a fence line there was a newborn calf on one side of the fence and its mother on the other side. The calf could have been a model for Charlie Russell's drawing, "Last of the 10,000." Its feet were caked in ice and the poor little guy could barely move. I helped the calf get through the fence where, hopefully, Mama could mother him up a bit. The cow and calf were on the same side of the fence now, but it seemed clear to me that the calf needed to get warm if it was going to have a chance at survival.

When I got back to the truck I drove up to the house and told the landowner's son, home for the holidays, about the calf and where it was.

That evening, the landowner phoned to thank me for alerting them about the calf. The calf spent the afternoon in the kitchen gradually warming up. By evening he was up on his feet and nursing on Mama. It looked like he was going to make it.

I was back at the ranch for a New Year's Eve day hunt, and after a trek through the willows and cattails, where we put up some pheasants and Huns, I stopped at the house to thank my friends for the opportunity to hunt on the ranch, and then asked how the calf was doing.

The calf had some residual frostbite damage on his back feet but otherwise was doing fairly well. The calf, it turned out, was a little heifer and they had named it Paula after me. A rare honor.

This fall, when I called for permission to hunt, I asked, "How is Paula, my calf, doing?" After a long pause, he said, "I'm afraid not too well. That frostbite damage was too severe. She couldn't get hooves to stay on her feet. We finally had to put her down."

If winter is a test of survival, it's truly a rude entry into the world for babies leaving the warm, wet tropical world of a mother's womb for a frozen, windswept foothill prairie. Some stories, unfortunately, don't have happy endings.

Golden Years, Golden Hours

Chapter 43

A Miracle Hunt

A covey of Hungarian partridge took to the air. The flush of Huns always startles me, even when I know they're around. A moment earlier I had seen them flush and go a short distance, and then saw them running along the edge of an old irrigation ditch. Any hopes that they would settle down and let me get in shotgun range were dashed when they again took off—this time for parts unknown.

I walked back down the hillside where my black Lab, Flicka, was working on another scent. While my back was turned, a larger group of partridge took off. Hungarian partridge, or, more accurately, European gray partridge, frustrate me, and they've been doing it for years.

Flicka ignored my frustrations and kept working her scent trail, following it to where the second bunch of Huns had flushed. I assumed she was following partridge scent, so when the cock pheasant flushed from the sagebrush it was a surprise, but not such a surprise that I forgot to shoot. I swung my gun along the bird's flight path and pulled the trigger, tumbling the pheasant.

Flicka made the retrieve and we continued our hunt. In a frozen, marshy creek bottom, another cock pheasant flushed from a patch of grass, again followed by a shot and a retrieve.

With two handsome, long-tailed pheasant roosters weighting down my vest, we'd had a successful hunt, especially for December.

The pheasants were a happy bonus to the hunt. Spending the chilly winter afternoon following Flicka through the sagebrush and creek bottom would have been enough—a miracle in itself.

Just two weeks earlier, on the day before Thanksgiving, we'd been out on a hunt. We were looking for ducks, and already had one mallard. Our next stop was a tract of public land along a busy highway where I occasionally find pheasants. While I put on my vest and loaded my shotgun for our walk, a person pulled in at some mailboxes on the other side of the road. Flicka charged across the road to check him out, and then started back to me.

It was one of those things you could see was going to happen, and there's nothing you can do about it. A car was coming and Flicka was in harm's way. After the collision Flicka shrieked in pain and surprise, then ran to me on her own power. I knelt down to comfort her, horrified at the encounter, expecting I might have to use my shotgun to end her suffering. After a moment, she settled down and was able to get in the truck without help. She had a bloody gash under her chin, but no other injuries that I could see. The driver of the car had stopped and I had a brief conversation with him. He had a broken grill on his car.

I called my wife and asked her to call our veterinarians and alert them to an incoming emergency, and then hit the road for home. After x-rays and several hours of observation, they sent her home. Aside from the gash on her chin, which the doctor sutured, and a bunch of bruises, Flicka apparently escaped major injury. We'd just have to keep her quiet for a week or so while she healed. We all agreed she was one lucky dog.

And that's why this afternoon's outing seemed like a miracle.

December is, of course, a season for miracles. In December we celebrate the miracle of Christmas. Jon Carroll, a columnist for the San Francisco *Chronicle*, makes it clear that he's not a religious believer, yet he loves to celebrate Christmas. We celebrate the birth of a child, he says. What's not to like about Christmas?

My wife and I are churchgoers, and that is where we celebrate the Christmas miracle. That year, though, we had new insights into miracles, when we consider a collision between a 75-pound Labrador retriever and a two-ton car, with the car ending up second best.

Nevertheless, while we believe in miracles, Flicka was on a leash for later stops along that highway. She also seemed to have a bit more respect for cars.

The wind was from the south, though there was no warmth in the gusting breezes. The air temperature was a crisp 5° above zero, not exactly warm, though not bad compared to the sub-zero temperatures of a week earlier. The snow was ankle deep and compacted from several days of drifting to make trudging through the snow tough going.

Late season hunting is often challenging, and generally the immediate challenge is just being out in the field in bitter winter weather, and that's after driving icy, snow-packed roads just to get to the hunting area.

Ducks were the main goal for this hunt, big, hardy mallards that don't worry about deep snow or sub-zero weather. They find food and a warm microclimate of sorts in warm water spring creeks on several ranches where I hunt this time of the year. There are no guarantees, of course, in that the ducks could just as easily have decided to quit fighting winter and go south where wheat and barley stubble fields aren't covered with snow.

On our first walk the creek was seemingly devoid of ducks, though the sound of a hen mallard quacking about 30 yards behind me told me I had just walked by a single duck hiding along the edge of the bank. I laughed at myself and wished the duck well as she flew off.

A couple weeks earlier, Flicka and I put up a few ducks, followed by a single hen mallard that flew just a short distance and then dropped into some grassy cover. I sent Flicka to find it. The bird again got up and flew a couple feet off the ground and then landed. If it had trouble flying, there was nothing wrong with her legs as she scampered across a plowed field, making sudden turns that once sent Flicka rolling in the dirt when she tried to make too tight a turn. Still, there was no doubt about the outcome of this race as Flicka finally caught up with the duck and brought it to me—without a shot being fired.

On the next creek, Flicka and I walked a long loop across a field to make an approach at a stretch of creek sheltered by a line of willows. There were occasional patches of snow covered with pheasant tracks, indicating where pheasants had been scratching in the snow to pick up grains of barley on the ground.

When we got to the creek a dozen mallards took to the air. I swung on the birds and shot twice. At first I thought I'd missed and then a drake mallard flew back towards the creek and dropped into brush on the other side of the water. Flicka looked for more birds to flush, but when no birds took to the air, she finally went across the creek and came back with the mallard firmly, but gently, in her mouth.

After we put this duck in my vest we continued our walk along the creek and pheasants started flushing from tall grass along the stream. Most of the pheasants we saw were hens, but I finally got a clear shot at a rooster and sent it tumbling into the powdery snow.

With a prime mallard duck and a pheasant in my vest I forgot about the cold and the wind. There are never guarantees with hunting, but with winter hunts the occasional rewards are all that much more treasured.

Golden Years, Golden Hours

Chapter 44

End of a Season

I love church potlucks but hate meetings, especially meetings about constitution and by-law changes, so after church, on this gray November day, I went home, changed clothes, made a sandwich and loaded up Flicka for an afternoon ruffed grouse hunt.

It's quite warm for early November, with temperatures hanging around 60° as we head for the hills, though the temperature is starting to drop as we start our walk up the mountainside. There's a forecast for a winter storm, so I'm wearing a polar fleece vest and a windbreaker over my shirt.

In the trees, the blustery wind isn't a problem and I quickly warm up as we walk up the mountainside.

It's a long climb through the aspen thickets, but we make it to the top of the aspens, where I sit down at the base of a tree and eat my sandwich and apple, sharing bites with Flicka. As we resume our walk down the hill there are a few drops of rain in the air.

When we are most of the way down the hill, where the aspen thickets level out, a grouse flushes wild from a clump of brush. All I can see of the bird is a flash of the grouse as it ghosts through the trees. Flicka runs off in pursuit and the bird flushes again and I see even less of it this time.

We head down the hill, hoping we'll flush the bird again. Flicka puts up the bird and I get two shots at it, and I think I might have dropped it on the second barrel. I get down to where I think it might have fallen and Flicka is already there, nuzzling the grouse, a nice-sized gray-phase ruffie..

There are watercress springs along the hillside and after I take a couple photos of Flicka and the grouse, I harvest a baggie of watercress. As we resume our walk the rain picks up and by the time we complete our circle of the covert and get back to the truck I feel rather damp and chilled. During our walk, I learn, the temperature has dropped down to the mid-40s.

It wasn't raining at home, however, though the weather system finally hits around 7 p.m., with rain that lasts several hours. The skies are clear when we go to bed that night, but in the morning there's an inch of snow on the ground and the temperature is 10°, and the forecast is for -20° F. by Wednesday.

Winter has arrived.

It's a mild morning for early December. In the last few weeks Flicka and I have gone out a couple times for waterfowl. We've gotten a couple ducks, though we haven't seen many numbers of ducks and geese

This morning our friend John has invited me for a pheasant hunt. John is a retired physician and for a number of years he and some friends, most of them also physicians, have leased hunting rights on a southwestern Montana ranch. In September, every year, they buy a couple hundred pheasants and release them in a portion of the property designated a preserve.

By December, a lot of the birds have succumbed, either to predators or doctors, and the survivors are thoroughly wild, though they still come back near the ranch buildings where the landowner scatters some chicken feed to encourage them to stay around.

Cows have grazed down much of the cover by this time of year, but in a patch that still has some tall grass Flicka puts up a pheasant. I drop it with my second shot from my 20-gauge over/under. "Great shot!" exclaims John.

We work into a frozen creek bottom with clumps of willows along the banks. Flicka goes on point. The bird flushes and I shoot and drop it. The bird hits the ground running, but Flicka is right on it and makes the retrieve. A couple minutes later I have a third rooster. "I tell John, 'I've got my limit. I'll start working on yours.'" He replies, "There is no limit!"

A bit further another pheasant flushes and Flicka and I again team up to get the bird. I'm relieved to see that we're not too far from the truck as four big pheasants in the back of my vest is getting to be a load.

By now, it's noon and we drive to another part of the ranch where we can get out of the wind and enjoy the thin warmth of the December sun. We've had a fun morning, with Flicka showing off, repeatedly, her skills as a pheasant dog. We cap off the afternoon with a fifth bird, before we head back home.

'Twas a couple nights before Christmas and all through the house not a creature was stirring, except for the writer pacing the floor, disturbing even the mouse.

"Will you shut down that computer and call it a night?" asked—

no, demanded, the writer's wife. Staying up late, staring at the computer, didn't seem normal. Now, if he had fallen asleep in the recliner while watching the Kumquat Bowl, or some other ridiculous football game, that would be more typical.

"I'm sorry, dear," the writer responded, sipping stale coffee. "I'm having a terrible time with my Christmas column. My deadline is tomorrow—and you know how the editor is when my copy is late."

"So why do you always wait until the last minute to get started? You've had all week."

"I was hoping to have more to write about," he responded sleepily.

"Write about your last hunting trip. Isn't that what you usually do?"

"I guess, now that you mention it." He sipped his coffee and added, "But it's easier when I have something positive to tell about. It's difficult when the trip is a failure."

"This certainly wasn't the first time you went hunting and didn't come home with any game. What's the big deal?"

The writer pondered her question as he poured himself another cup of coffee and mentally reviewed that last pheasant outing.

It was a mild morning when he left to hunt a ranch an hour's drive away. It was a ranch he usually put off hunting until the late season because the pheasants generally hang out in this big, marshy creek bottom, with thick willows along the creek, with patches of cattails and marsh grass. There are springs that feed the marsh and he liked to wait until cold weather froze all the water and it would be easier to get around.

East of the Continental Divide the weather looked nice, with bright sunshine reflecting off the snow. The wind, however, was roaring down the eastern slopes. The snow was crusted from recent thaws; otherwise there would be a lot of drifting.

He trudged through sagebrush above the creek, noting pheasant tracks in the snow. The birds are around, he thought, and they've been out feeding. With the wind, he figured the pheasants would be in heavier cover. With his black Lab leading the way he wandered around in the tangled willows and other trees before coming out to the marshy area. He hadn't gone far when he broke through the ice and water seeped in over his boot tops.

The treacherous ice didn't bother the dog. She scampered across the marsh, plowing her way through the cattails, and then went into a big patch of tall grasses next to the creek. A whitetail buck scampered out, followed by a hen pheasant flying to safety, and then a doe and half-grown fawn.

He tried to work himself to where the dog was, but the brush was too thick to get through. The dog put up a few more pheasants from inside the willows. All he could do was think bad thoughts as he heard pheasants fly away. Finally, after slipping on some solid ice, making a hard landing on his hip and elbow, and following that with breaking through more ice, he decided that this trip wasn't much fun. He and his puzzled dog limped back through the snow to the truck and went home.

Telling the story to his wife he concluded, "See? That's not much to write about."

The wife smiled consolingly, but reminded him, "So it wasn't your best hunt. So what! Just think how lucky you are. You have good places to hunt. You put up some pheasants and you saw lots of other wildlife. It's Christmas time and you've been hunting since the beginning of September. We have game in the freezer.

"Why don't you just write that you're having a good hunting season and wish everybody a Merry Christmas? It can't be that difficult."

And so the house eventually grew quiet, though the mouse wondered, "So what was all that about?"

A week later Flicka and I are out for another hunt on a small ranch less than a half hour from home. We've had mild weather for the week before Christmas, and there's just a dusting of snow in sheltered areas where we find a few pheasant tracks.

The heart of pheasant habitat on the ranch is a long, brushy creek bottom, with big patches of cattails and marshes, with springs here and there. It's difficult walking, with patches of ice that can be treacherous walking, especially with a light dusting of snow, or, almost as bad, too thin to support my weight. Still, you have to go where the pheasants are—or should be.

Today, our walk results with just a hen pheasant flushing from a patch of sagebrush.

We trudge up a hillside where an old irrigation ditch follows the contours around the hill, and there are clumps of brush and trees where we've occasionally put up pheasants.

We don't see any pheasants though we do put up a covey of Hungarian partridge (or European gray partridge if you prefer). They're kind of at the edge of shooting range but I get off two shots at a rapidly disappearing bird and I have a hunch I knocked it down on the second barrel

Then I see it struggling up the hillside, trying without success to take to the air. It probably has a broken wing. I urge Flicka to search for the scent and to catch up with the bird. She picks up the scent and follows it up over the top of the hill. She returns a couple minutes later with the bird in her mouth.

I'm pleased with the partridge. It's the first and likely the only partridge of the season and I could use a fresh partridge skin for fly-tying, as well as a partridge for a future dinner.

We put up another hen pheasant on our circle back to the truck, but we have no more shooting action. At the end of the afternoon I'm also concerned about Flicka. She's been limping a bit this past week, favoring her left rear leg. At the end of today's hunt she's noticeably limping more.

We didn't go out on another hunt until a full month later. Usually we might have had at least several more late season hunts at the

tail end of the upland and waterfowl seasons. We had taken Flicka
to see her veterinarian about her leg and she confirmed our fears that
she might have damaged her knee. She suggested that we keep Flicka
relatively quiet for a few weeks to give her knee a chance to heal up.

Our last hunt of the season was more to make the rounds of the
several ranches where I hunt ducks and to express my appreciation for
their hospitality. The weather had been relatively warm and I wasn't
really expecting to find any ducks.

My suspicions turn out to be right on, and in more ways than one
our hunting season limped to an end.

I noted in my hunting journal my fears about Flicka's hunting
future and whether her career might soon be over. Back at the time
we got her in 2005 I wondered if she might turn out to be my last
hunting dog. Now, almost ten years later, new and difficult questions
come to the fore.

Golden Years, Golden Hours

Chapter 45

A Day out of Kilter

It was a sunny though chilly April day on the upper Big Hole River. The river, as usual, is beautiful. After a week of cold weather, spring runoff was on hold and the river was running low and clear as I stepped into the edge of the river and started drifting nymphs through the currents.

I wasn't sure I wanted to be fishing. My heart certainly wasn't into it, but I needed some solitude and peace to collect my thoughts and get my head tied back on straight.

The day felt out of kilter. I didn't start the day taking Flicka out to go potty, listening for new bird sounds as the spring migrations continue. When I started making a sandwich that morning I didn't have Flicka at my side, getting excited about an outing, and looking for tidbits of cheese or salami.

It struck me, in fact, that this was one of just a few outings in the last 45 years when I didn't have a Labrador retriever at my side.

Several days earlier, Flicka had been out playing with our neighbor's dog when she suddenly pulled up lame. Old football players have their trick knees, and old hunting dogs do, too. At the end of the last hunting season Flicka's left knee was getting gimpy, so we mostly took the last few weeks off from hunting to let it recover. Still, the last couple months she had been limping, especially after any kind of exercise. This time, however, she was holding up her right back leg, unable to put any weight on it.

With one bad leg we thought we could retire her from hunting, as difficult as it would be on Flicka, a dog truly born to hunt. With two bad legs she was suddenly a cripple—clearly in pain and misery. There are surgical procedures for ACL repair, but fixing two knees would mean six months of pain and hobbling. We could give her additional medication for pain management, though that wouldn't solve any problems.

Growing up on a farm with all sorts of animals around, a basic principle I learned from my dad was, "Don't let the poor thing suffer."

With a heavy heart I made an appointment with our veterinarian. We had a good discussion with Flicka's doctor, who mostly confirmed our diagnoses and options, and after giving us some private time to say our goodbyes, she gently helped Flicka along her way, my wife and I caressing Flicka as she peacefully drifted off into that final sleep.

I'm afraid we were wrecks the rest of the day. After several sleepless nights and days of emotional turmoil we felt exhausted and emotionally drained. In the morning, however, after finally getting a decent night's sleep, we felt rested, feeling comforted that, hard as it was, we had done the right thing for our beloved Flicka.

The reality is that when we get that chubby puppy we do so with the almost certain knowledge that at some point they're going to break our hearts. We had hoped that the inevitable might have been a few more years into the future, but reality got in the way.

As hard as it has been to say farewell to Flicka, knowing she had a great life as a pet and a wonderful hunting and fishing partner comforts us. She truly lived the life of a Labrador retriever. As our son, Kevin, commented, "She was phenomenal. Every time we hunted she'd put on a clinic on how to find pheasants." My Hoosier buddy, Charley, who joined us last September for several days of grouse hunting and fly-fishing, wrote, "I feel honored that I got to both hunt and fish with Flicka."

Back on the river, after a couple hours with no fish action I was ready to call it a day when a fish suddenly grabbed a dry fly. A minute later I landed my first Big Hole fish of the year, a pretty 10-inch grayling.

Our Big Hole arctic grayling have suffered through drought, land use changes, lawsuits, and politics and, yet, they hang on, and so will we. There will be a new chapter in our lives in the outdoors.

Chapter 46

Fishing and Hunting Through My Old Age Crisis

Howell Raines, a renowned journalist, who earned a lasting fame of sorts for being fired from his job as executive editor of the *New York Times*, also won recognition for other accomplishments, including writing about fly-fishing in his best-selling book, *Fly Fishing Through the Midlife Crisis*.

It was a good concept, one that I might have wished having first, other than the fact that it seemed I was too busy working and being involved with family to have a midlife crisis.

Now, I'm way too old to have one.

I'm not complaining. I feel extremely fortunate, actually. In my late 70s, I'm still fly-fishing and wading the Big Hole River, a trout stream that's known for dumping careless anglers. Besides fishing, I play tennis several times a week through the summer. When autumn comes you can find me wandering mountainside aspen thickets in search of ruffed grouse, and in October, there's no place I'd rather be than on a windy prairie, encouraging my Lab to find another pheasant.

Life is good, though there's no way around the inescapable reality that there are way more hunting and fishing seasons in my past than I can imagine having in my future.

Saying goodbye to Flicka, and that's now several years ago, was one of the most devastating times of my life. I just wasn't ready to let her go, even though it seemed the only realistic option to take.

At the same time, we had to move on, even when I wasn't ready. The same day we lost Flicka, our son, Kevin, sent me an email with a link to an online ad for a litter of Labrador retriever puppies. He was half-apologetic, saying, "Maybe you're not ready yet, but…"

Yes, that was a big but. I picked up the phone and talked to the breeder, an airman stationed at the Air Force base at Minot, North Dakota. He owned both of the puppies' parents and described them as great hunters. I told him to put my name on a black female pup and I put a deposit in the mail.

The several weeks between losing Flicka and getting the new puppy were difficult. We were grieving for Flicka and at the same time anxious to meet the pup.

On a warm, sunny day, I was playing tennis one morning when it seemed like I felt funky. My heart seemed to be racing and when I went to bed that night it seemed like my pulse was absolutely pounding. In the morning I told my wife that I better see a doctor.

The doctor quickly diagnosed what was happening as an "atrial flutter," a form of atrial fibrillation. He prescribed a medication to slow things down and referred me to a cardiologist for a follow-up.

Happily, everything turned out fine. The medication slowed

things back to normal. The cardiologist ran me through the full diagnostics of echocardiogram, stress test, and wearing a heart monitor for a couple days. I got a clean bill of health, and I haven't had any further episodes of atrial flutter.

Looking back, I'm totally convinced my episode of atrial flutter was caused by emotional stress, that emotional roller coaster of grief, on the one hand, and the anticipation of starting all over with a new puppy on the other.

We've now celebrated that puppy's fourth birthday. I can't believe how the time goes so quickly.

I can't help but speculate whether that puppy, now the veteran of four full seasons of chasing grouse, pheasants and ducks, along with swimming my trout waters, will be our last dog, but we're not going to look too far in the future.

On the other hand, the Minneapolis *StarTribune* recently ran a story by the *Strib*'s outdoor editor, Dennis Anderson, about Bud Grant, the former coach of the Minnesota Vikings football team. Bud Grant was a legendary coach in both the Canadian Football League and the National Football League, but football was always a job for Grant. His real passion was the outdoors. Even in the heat of a football season he'd find a way to go hunting almost every week.

Grant, at the time the article came out, was almost 90 years old, and the article told about him hunting ducks in Manitoba last fall, just him and his dog, and discovering, after a great hunt, that his Labrador retriever had a bunch of lumps that turned out to be cancerous. That turned out to be his dog's last hunt and Grant mercifully chose to not let his dog suffer.

Now, Grant is looking for a new Lab, though this time he's looking for an older, trained dog.

I couldn't ask for a better role model than Bud Grant, and good Lord willing, I'll still be hunting and fishing, with a Labrador retriever, or other such bird dog, at my side, when I'm his age.

Still, the odds are against it.

My wife and I went to our college class 55-year reunion a couple years ago. Part of the reunion festivities is a memorial service where we remember and honor classmates who have died in that half-century plus five since we put on caps and gowns for that graduation day academic procession.

About one-third of our graduating class has marched off in that final procession and as we reach our late 70s the inevitable reality is that most of the rest of us aren't far behind. In fact, on that reunion weekend some people were unable to attend because they were already on their deathbeds and died within a few months.

Yes, if we were inclined toward getting depressed about these things, we could, no doubt, find all sorts of grim statistics and prognostications about the realities of these coming years.

On the other hand, I don't have time for that kind of nonsense. Somehow, my life is highly scheduled and full of deadlines.

For example, I have a Kiwanis meeting every Tuesday at noon. On Wednesday afternoons I usually have a bridge game. On Thursdays, during school months, I go to a Key Club meeting. Key Club is a high school service club under the umbrella of Kiwanis International and I'm a Kiwanis advisor. During summer months, I play tennis on Monday, Tuesday and Thursday mornings. Somewhere I have to find time to write a weekly outdoors column for a local newspaper.

During much of the year I have weekly rehearsals with our community symphony orchestra, where I play a French horn, which further means I have to carve out some practice time most every day. Right now I've just finished the final year of a three-year term on the board of directors of the Outdoor Writers Association of America.

Friday is usually my "play day," a day that I generally reserve for getting out of town to go fishing, hunting, or skiing, depending on the season. During warm weather months, we'll often start the weekend early, hooking up our camping trailer on Thursday afternoon and heading for a trout stream.

When we're not traveling or camping on weekends, my wife and

I attend church on Sunday mornings. In addition both my wife and I have church activities and commitments.

Our adult children occasionally question why I, supposedly retired, have let myself get so tied down. I always smile and confess it's all my fault, but keeping myself busy with commitments and having a regular routine is one of the ways I stay young, or at least not let myself drift off into some sort of aimless existence, which is all too often the reality for people my age.

In short, we, meaning both my wife and I, have anchors in our lives. We have commitments, we see other people, we have an active religious life, and we're involved with community activities, often activities that keep us connected with people of a wide range of ages.

We find time for recreation, whether it's mentally stimulating, such as playing bridge or a musical instrument, or that involves physical activity, plus we find time for recreation that keeps us connected with the outdoors, whether it's camping along a trout stream, fly-fishing, or following a bird dog and carrying a shotgun.

Obviously, none of those things will keep the Grim Reaper from someday showing up at my door. As other observers have noted, the only sure thing in life is that we don't get out of it alive. But, if we stay active and involved, hopefully we'll continue to have a full and rewarding life as long as possible.

Golden Years, Golden Hours

Chapter 47

On Being a "Senior Citizen"

"I've got a question," the caller said. This was back when I was manager of the local Social Security office. "When do people become senior citizens?"

I chuckled at his question and told him there's no quick and easy answer. "AARP starts sending you mail when you hit 50. Some fast food places give you a senior citizen's discount when you're 50 or 55. You can get Social Security checks when you're 62. On the other hand, Big Sky ski resort doesn't give you a senior citizen discount until you're 70."

"Yeah, but when are they officially senior citizens?" The poor guy thought he could get an official answer from the federal government and all I could do was give him another run-around.

Our concepts of aging have changed. It is probably more a case that when we're young we have misconceptions about the aging process and as we go through it ourselves, we throw many of those silly ideas out the window.

As a kid, any thoughts I had about people in their 60s was, "Wow, they're old. Heck, they're even older than my parents are, and they're ancient." Actually, when I look back, some of those "Senior Citizens" from my youth were old. After a lifetime of strenuous labor and living through hard times such as the Depression years, many people were seemingly worn out by the time they reached their 60s.

Now I look at people in their 60s and 70s, and, yes, 80s, and they are leading active lives. They play golf, play tennis, go skiing (and ski black diamond runs), and look good doing it.

Having the right genes is an asset if you're hung up on looks. In my case, I reached a milestone of sorts when I was about 45 and stopped at the store on a spring day to buy my fishing license. The young woman at the counter was filling out the form, asking me questions, but when she came to hair color, she glanced up and wrote down "Gray" before I had a chance to tell her my hair was brown.

It all happens fast, if you think about it.

A few years earlier, when I was still a lad in my early 20s, it seemed I was always the youngest looking person in any group, and often the youngest in years as well. I vividly remember Christine, an elementary school teacher who wanted some projections on Social Security benefits. She was disappointed with the information I gave her and told me, "You're too young to know anything." I felt insulted, though in looking back I probably was too young, even if the information I gave Christine was correct.

I was last carded in a bar when I was 30.

So, there it is. In my 20s, I was too young to know anything, and at 30, still suspiciously young-looking to be in a bar. At 45, I was gray and middle-aged. Now, I look at myself in a mirror and wish that I could keep my thinning gray hair on the top of my head a little longer, and that seems to be just that: wishful thinking.

Something I noticed when we hit our 40s was that we started going to funerals. First we said goodbye to parents and others from an earlier generation. Then we started saying goodbye to people my own age and younger. There were some accidental deaths in there, but usually it was people my age and younger who were dying from cancer and heart attacks. By the time I got into my 50s I began to feel like a survivor, and now that I'm in my late 70s, I know darn well that I'm a survivor.

When I turned 60, I did some self-examination. I asked myself, "What do I plan to be doing when I'm 70 or more?" I decided I wanted to be flyfishing on the Big Hole River, hunting pheasants, playing tennis and…a few other things as well.

The first step to doing all that at 70 and older is to be doing it at 60, and start doing those things before age 50. If you're already in your 70s, it might be a little late to start creating a lifestyle.

Now that I'm 80, I look back and determine with some satisfaction that the plan worked.

But, getting back to that original question about when do we become a senior citizen, my thought is, not yet. Old grouch? Yeah, I can't argue with that, but senior citizen? Not yet.

Golden Years, Golden Hours

Chapter 48

Get an Early Start*
*So you can go back and get what
you forgot

It was a beautiful autumn day, this Veterans Day holiday, several years ago. I decided it would be a good afternoon to head to the hills for an afternoon of ruffed grouse hunting. Naturally, Flicka, our black Labrador retriever, agreed with this notion.

I had an early lunch at home, put on my hunting clothes and grabbed a shotgun, loaded up the truck and we headed for the hills.

We got to a favorite spot, parked, put on my shell vest, making sure I had shells for the afternoon hunt. Meanwhile, Flicka was dancing around, barking at me, clearly communicating, "Come on! Let's go! It'll be so much fun!"

Finally, I grab my shotgun and I'm ready to cross the creek at the side of the road when I break open the action and realize that I'd brought my 20-gauge over/under shotgun. In a better world, this wouldn't be a problem, except for the fact that the only shells I had with me were 28-gauge.

I went back to the truck to double check what I already knew; there were no 20-gauge shotgun shells in the truck.

I weighed my options. I could go home and trade guns, but by the time I did the almost hour and a half round trip there wouldn't be much time left for hunting. I finally decided to make the best of it where I was. I put the gun back in the truck and grabbed a plastic bag and hiked into the aspens to a hillside spring where a bountiful crop of watercress grows. I picked a bag of watercress while Flicka checked the trees and brushy thickets for grouse.

I got a watercress salad, or three, out of the deal and Flicka got some healthy exercise, even if she didn't quite understand why I wasn't toting a shotgun and why we had to go back home so soon. Of course, after getting home I kicked myself again. There is another town just 10 miles from my hunting spot. I could have made a relatively quick trip to get 20-gauge shells there.

After a service club meeting the next day we went back to the covert and this time I had the right gun. As the afternoon turned out, however, I had a shot at just one grouse—and missed. It seems I did just as well not carrying a gun.

This, of course, isn't the first time I've brought the wrong gun. A few years earlier I went on a similar ruffed grouse outing, and when I put a 20-gauge shell in the gun it dropped through the chamber and lodged halfway down the barrel. I'd grabbed my 12-gauge shotgun instead of the 20.

That time I'd also taken along a handsaw. Some woodcutters had been cutting firewood in the area, so I took a saw along to scavenge some firewood. It wasn't a wasted afternoon. I came home without any birds, though with more firewood than expected.

I could blame old age, though the truth is that I've been forgetting things crucial to fishing or hunting outings for years. I hate to think how often I've just gotten on the road, or gotten to my destination, and realized I'd forgotten a shotgun, or shell vest, fishing vest, license, boots, or any of a dozen other doohickeys.

When I'm lucky I think of it shortly after I leave home, though there certainly have been a number of times when I've gotten to my destination at a trout stream or hunting spot, discovered what I'd forgotten, and made a round trip back home, where I'd pop in the house and make a sheepish confession to my wife, and quickly retreat to the sound of laughter.

Sometimes it can work out to be a positive experience. On one of those occasions I'd gone fishing without bringing along my vest, I decided to make the best of it and just go fishing.

I had a fly-box in the back of the truck filled with mostly big salmon fly imitations, though with some smaller, more generic flies. I had a spare tippet spool as well, so I had the essentials. In a pinch, you can use a bit of lip balm as a fly floatant. Looking back, I think I had a pretty successful day of fly-fishing, and actually enjoyed the feeling of not being weighted down with a vest that's typically overstuffed with things I don't often use, but think I have to have.

Of course, something I didn't have was the fishing license sitting back home in the vest. Fortunately, no game wardens came around, so I got away with it that time.

Not long after that I picked up a mini-chest pack that's big enough to hold a small fly-box and some floatant, and has clips for a nipper and forceps. It's just about right for a quiet evening.

When I'm packed for an outing, I usually go through a little mental checklist. For fishing, it'll go, "Waders, gaiters, boots, vest." For hunting, it's "Guns, shells, vest, whistle," or to that effect.

The awkward time comes, usually, in early autumn when I go out for either a day of hunting or fishing, forgetting what I did the previous trip, and end up on the bank of the river remembering that my license (same piece of paper for both hunting and fishing) is in my hunting vest, or vice versa. On one of those occasions I stopped at a fly-shop and purchased a duplicate license, figuring that the $5 fee was cheaper than the gas I'd burn up going home and back.

In most years I do some hunting and fishing in North Dakota, a state that has gone to a totally online licensing system, and you can print off as many copies of your license as you like. Montana's system isn't quite there yet, though I can get my basic licenses online, and I do print multiple copies for various vests and jackets.

I'll again confess that I really can't blame old age for forgetting stuff. My history goes back too far for that.

A prime example is the time, in the 1960s, that three of us, coworkers at our office in Fargo, North Dakota, put in for antelope tags. We were successful in the drawing and we prepared our checklists of all the stuff we needed for a long weekend of hunting antelope and sharp-tailed grouse, and camping at the other end of the state. The evening for hitting the road, we gathered at Larry's house to pack everything in his car (this was the era before SUVs, and Larry's Chevy had a cavernous trunk, and, yes, we hit the road in the middle of the night—Larry liked to drive at night). A few blocks from Larry's house my wife asked, a bit facetiously, "You've got everything? Got your gun?"

Bingo! I had a lot of stuff but I'd forgotten the rifle and shotgun at home. We made a quick turnaround for the guns. Nobody was the wiser.

I guess I'm not the only one to forget things. I once wrote a newspaper column about my tendency to forget things. A veteran and now-retired local game warden sent me an email commenting to the effect of, "Don't feel bad. Some of the people I come across are so clueless I'm surprised they even know how to walk."

Chapter 49

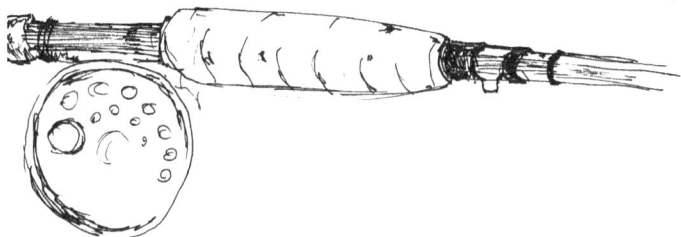

What the Hell! It's Just Money

The reality that the future isn't as far off as it used to be isn't as bad as you might guess.

A few years back a former columnist for *Gun Dog* magazine told of growing up in rural Canada during the Depression years. Money was tight and there was little to spare for recreation. Still, the author's father would sometimes have some loose change that he thought could be spent on hunting grouse. At least, there would be the possibility that money spent on shotgun shells could end up as dinner for a hungry family.

So, on those occasions, the father would give his son a quarter and instruct him to walk to the hardware store in town and buy five shotgun shells, at a nickel apiece.

Fast forwarding to near-present times, the columnist wrote about going on a waterfowl hunt and stocking up on expensive non-steel, non-toxic magnum load shotgun shells that were sold in boxes of ten shells and would cost somewhere in the neighborhood of five dollars per shell.

He contemplated the purchase of these expensive shotgun shells, reflecting back on his Depression Era boyhood and buying shotgun shells for his father at five cents apiece and then concluded, "What the hell, it's just money," and plunked down the money (or more likely, credit card) and bought the shells.

I'm a Depression kid, also, though I was born in 1939, just before the beginning of the war that would boost the country back to prosperity. Still, I grew up learning my parents' attitudes about thrift and saving, lessons they learned the hard way during those hard times.

Now, after living many years, we've reached a point in life when we can realistically figure that our financial savings could well outlive us, and it's a liberating concept. It's never a sure thing, of course. If I or my wife, or both of us, should end up in a nursing home, it's a given that in a relatively short time those savings will be gone and we'll be relying on Medicaid to pay the brunt of our care, and if we have our senses about us, we'll occasionally express thoughts of gratitude to our younger fellow citizens whose taxes will be financing a portion of our miserable existence.

I won't even feel guilty. I have been a responsible taxpayer all my adult life and bear no grudges that a few cents from my tax dollars have been financing the care of others. Still, we're hoping that we'll be able to avoid the unattractive option of custodial care. I will, however, point out that my wife worked a number of years as a nursing home social worker and we're in agreement that if a time comes that nursing home care is needed we'll do the right thing and place the needy person into appropriate care, and we've promised each other to never promise that we won't do that.

But, enough of this nonsense! We're in good health and plan to stay that way and continue to live active lives.

Active lives mean, of course, active outdoor lives.

Active outdoor lives involve toys of one kind or another. In my case, my choice of toys usually involves fly rods or shotguns.

In my discussion of shotguns in an earlier chapter I mentioned that my loving wife, after being called back to work for a few months, generously suggested I buy that new shotgun I'd been drooling over. That shotgun turned out to be a 28-gauge, and it has been a pleasure to carry it across my mountain aspen thickets and prairie pheasant habitats. It's relatively light and when I do my job, it does its job, and birds tend to drop to the ground, on their way to our dinner table.

On the other hand, the problem with a 28-gauge shotgun is that you're almost guaranteed to never find shotgun shells for sale at a loss leader price. For that matter, you have to make sure, when you go off on a hunting trip, that you have more than enough shotgun shells for the duration, as it's a just about sure thing that you won't be able to find 28-gauge shells in small town hardware stores.

Fly rods? I've had a long fascination with bamboo fly rods. Back in the time when I was born, fly rods, most fishing rods, for that matter, were synonymous with bamboo rods.

In the years after World War II, fiberglass came along and technology pushed fishing pole developments for many years, as graphite and boron variations of fiberglass became the standard fishing rod, for fly-fishing and other variations on casting lures or bait.

Still, some rod-makers persisted in crafting bamboo fly rods for a selective market of people who prefer to fish with bamboo. In fact, right now we're having a renaissance of sorts, as many people have taken up the challenge of crafting bamboo fly rods. Glenn Brackett, whom I profile here, recently made a presentation to the local chapter of Trout Unlimited, saying that there are now some 10,000 people, many of them hobbyists, building bamboo fly rods in the U.S.," adding, "I have helped many of them."

Glenn Brackett lives in Butte, Montana now, but grew up in the

San Francisco area where he learned the art of crafting bamboo fly rods for the R. L. Winston Rod Co., eventually becoming a co-owner of the company. He and his partner, Tom Morgan, moved the company from California to the small town of Twin Bridges, Montana.

They later sold the company, though Glenn continued to run the bamboo rod shop for Winston, and trained others in the zen-like art of building bamboo rods, including Jerry Kustich, a friend and writer as well. It's a long story, but around a dozen years ago, Glenn had a falling out with Winston and he and Jerry launched a new bamboo rod business, Sweetgrass Rods, at another facility in Twin Bridges.

Several years ago, I approached the 75-year milestone and I decided that in honor of this occasion I should have a new fly rod, and this one would be a Sweetgrass bamboo rod.

I already had a couple bamboo rods. My first was kind of a rehabilitation project. A co-worker, Glenn, had picked up a bamboo rod that had been confiscated, for some reason, at the U.S./Canadian border, and was sold at auction. A few years later he said he was going to sell it at a garage sale and asked if I had suggestions for what to ask for it. I said I'd be right over to check it out.

It was pretty sad, with windings on the guides fraying, and the tip section shattered. I said, "I'll give you five bucks for it." Glenn looked pretty disappointed but we made the deal. It was like I once read about real bargaining; when both parties to a transaction walk away from the deal feeling cheated.

That rod was a winter project. I found a book at the public library with instructions on how to repair that shattered tip section. I stripped off the guides and basically rebuilt the rod. The following summer I took it with me on our summer vacation trip to Montana and caught a few fish with it, though it became clear that casting with this rod was like waving a telephone pole. It was a really heavy and clunky casting tool.

A few years later, after retiring from my government career and reinventing myself as a writer, I wrote a story about a resident of Ennis,

Montana, who had been a bamboo rod collector. He finally settled in Ennis and rented a storefront to make money selling off his collection. I brought my rod with me for an evaluation.

He looked at my rod and said, "These rods were brought in from Japan after the war (WWII) by the old Western Auto hardware chain." Looking at the repaired tip section and my re-building job, he added, "It might be worth five bucks. Now, they were shipped in a teak box. If you had that, it'd really be worth something."

I have another bamboo rod that was something of a fluke. Our daughter, Erin, was taking her dog for a walk in her neighborhood in the hills of Oakland, California. She spotted what looked like an aluminum rod case sticking out of a garbage can on the curb, waiting for pickup. She decided that it merited further inspection so she picked it up and brought it home. A couple months later she came to Montana for Thanksgiving, bringing it along. In the rod case was a bamboo rod of sorts. There was an English-made Cortland bamboo rod butt section, along with a mismatched tip section. The inscription on the rod butt said it was an 8-foot, 8-weight rod, kind of an unusual version.

I took it to Sweetgrass Rods to see if something could be done with it, and the bamboo guys in Twin Bridges referred it to Glenn. He called me up and said he could build a new tip section for it and quoted a price that seemed more than reasonable.

A couple months later he called to say the job was done, and I went to his house, where he has a bamboo rod shop in the garage. He had done a beautiful job of building the new tip section to match the butt section. He built a new taper to the tip section to lighten the action so it was more like a 7-weight.

We had a cup of tea and a long chat about rods and fishing, including a tantalizing bit of history. When he was with the Winston Company in San Francisco, there was a retail shop in the front of the building and Cortland bamboo rods were among the models they sold. So, there was the intriguing, if remote, possibility that he had originally sold this Cortland rod in San Francisco, and now he completed a job to rebuild and restore it. We'll never know, but it's possible.

In any event, as my 75-year birthday year came around, I suggested to my wife that I had an idea for something of a splurge for Father's Day, a Sweetgrass bamboo rod. Bless this beautiful woman's heart, she gave her okay.

In June 2014, I drove to Twin Bridges and tried out several bamboo rods and drove home, an hour later, with a 4/5-weight pentagonal bamboo rod. It's pentagonal, meaning it was built with five strips of bamboo. Most bamboo rods, these days, are built with six strips, so it's just a bit unique, though not to Sweetgrass.

This past year, Glenn Brackett closed his Twin Bridges facility and moved Sweetgrass Rods to a new shop in Butte. Things change, but I'm glad that I was in a position that I could buy a handcrafted bamboo fly rod coming from one of today's master craftsmen. Glenn didn't build it, but, assuredly, it met his approval before it went into inventory.

I suppose I could have some second thoughts about splurging for a bamboo rod from a prestigious rod maker's shop. I could have purchased a couple high-end graphite rods for the same price, or a whole handful of inexpensive fly rods from a big box store. Heaven knows a $40 rod from big box mart will catch just as many trout as a handcrafted bamboo rod. The trout don't care. For that matter, in coming years, my son, Kevin, will most likely get more use out of my Sweetgrass rod than I ever will, just as he'll likely also end up with my 28-gauge shotgun.

But, what the hell! It's just money.

What the Hell! It's Just Money

Chapter 50

A Happy Beginning to Life

I occasionally look back at what is turning out to be a long life and have to pinch myself once in a while to realize that all the adventures of a lifetime actually happened. I didn't just imagine it.

I was a child of the Depression, and grew up on a small farm where our family worked hard to make it successful. My first years of public education were in a one-room country school. Most of the time I was the only person in my grade, so I spent a lot of time listening to other children getting instruction, or doing a lot of reading on my own.

There were a couple glass-front bookcases in the back of the schoolroom and there was an encyclopedia on one shelf, and a couple gems of literature, including Mark Twain's *Tom Sawyer*, which became a lifetime favorite.

The school, which was a quarter-mile walk from our farm, was on a one-acre plot of land, next to a cow pasture. On one side of the school there was a playground of sorts, with a slide, swings, and a teeter-totter. There were two outhouses in back of the school building.

On the other side of the school was our sports field, so to speak. We had a basketball hoop, and we'd often have basketball games with whatever numbers of kids were on hand to form teams. If there were just a couple we'd play "horse," trying to match basketball shots.

Beyond the hoop was our softball field, and during the spring we'd play ball during recesses and noon breaks. There were never enough boys to form teams, so we'd play "workup," with the slowest person to call for a position playing the outfield, working our way up to become the batter, hoping we wouldn't strike out or pop up on our first at-bat, and have to go right back to the outfield.

In the fall, we'd play touch football, perhaps imagining that, one day, we'd play for the high school football team when we went to "town school," or even the Minnesota Golden Gophers under Coach Bernie Bierman.

In some winters, that athletic field often had deep snowdrifts, and we'd dig tunnels in the drifts during recess. One year, one of the other boys brought a carton of ice cream from home and we ate ice cream way back in the snow tunnels. I remember it as one of the best treats of those years.

We didn't have much in the line of sophisticated learning aids. The school subscribed to school-oriented newspapers, which came under the topic of "current events," or "curnievents," as I long thought it was. I'm embarrassed to recall that, in looking at a photo of then Secretary of State Dean Acheson, in that time of rampant McCarthyism, some of us solemnly agreed that, "He sure looks like a Communist."

On the other hand, there was a piano in the school and we always had several kids who could play it, having taken piano lessons from my mother. We'd have sing-alongs, often learning songs that would never survive in today's schools, such as "Old Black Joe," or "Dixie."

Once or twice a year we'd have a school play, or "program," as we called it. We'd rig up a stage with planks on sawhorses, and we'd improvise stage curtains with sheets on a wire strung across the room. We'd perform our program for our parents and families, and most people brought food for a big lunch after the performance.

We didn't have much at the school, compared to the computers, internet, and other sophisticated teaching devices modern schools take for granted, though some things were priceless. In that cow pasture behind the school property was a little creek, in fact, the same creek that ran through the middle of our farm, two properties upstream from school. In the spring, wild flowers would bloom in the pasture. One memorable day, we had a mud ball fight along the creek. I don't know what modern parents might say about such activity. If my parents ever knew about it, they didn't say anything. I guess a kid coming home with muddy shirt and pants wasn't all that unusual.

Many people, looking back at educations in one-room country schools, tend to idealize the experience, thinking they got a superior education. I'm not sure I'd go that far. I know I missed out on a lot of social interaction with people my age, and I definitely didn't learn what it meant to compete in the classroom. Still, I have no regrets. I learned my 3-Rs. I had the advantage of listening in on classes above me and often could participate. Probably the greatest gift of those six years is my lifelong love of reading.

Most of my fellow students did well when we finished our country school years and went on to town school. Even with late starts, we got into band, sang in chorus, and other activities, and some were star athletes in high school. I played football, but I spent most games warming the bench. I even remember a few of them as homecoming royalty, and in a small town high school it doesn't get much better than that.

Growing up on a farm, going to a country school, and being outside in all kinds of weather, whether for work or play, certainly created an outdoors-oriented mindset. I had the freedom, much of the time, to wander the farm, with its pond and creek, catch tiny fish in pools, catch frogs, observe migrating waterfowl, and all the other things a kid with an imagination might do. At various times I might have been a cowboy, or Daniel Boone, or an Indian warrior. Alas, as I got a little older, some of that freedom was curtailed a bit for the sake of driving a tractor, cultivating corn, baling hay, and livestock chores.

Richard Louv wrote the book, *Last Child in the Woods*, lamenting the diminished opportunities for today's children to just wander in the outdoors, without adults hovering over them. The kids of my generation could have been prime examples of the positive impacts of growing up around nature.

When wandering around I might be carrying a fishing rod of sorts, a bow and arrow, or the .22 rifle I found under the Christmas tree when I was around 11 years old. When I was 15, I talked my parents into letting me try pheasant hunting. My mother took me to town, one Saturday morning, where we went into the local Gamble's store, where a sales person took down a 12 gauge single-shot shotgun from a rack, put a box of shotgun shells next to it, filled out a hunting license, and my mother wrote a check for something like $25. The pheasant season opened at noon, and at the stroke of the hour I walked out the backdoor of the farmhouse for my first pheasant hunt.

It was a modest start, one that did not result in a pheasant dinner, but over 60 years later I still get excited when I go out for a pheasant hunt, and I am still thrilled, and sometimes bone-shaking startled, when a pheasant rooster gets up at my feet. I'm still thrilled about cooking pheasant dinners.

I could go on and on about other aspects of growing up when I did, when radio was still in its golden age, or of a few years later, the golden age of early television, when most programming was live. I'll just mention that coming home from school in the afternoon and listening to radio programs such as "Sergeant Preston of the Yukon," "Superman," "The Lone Ranger," or "Straight Arrow," all using that marvelous theater of the mind that was radio drama, is a treasured memory, and that was just for starters.

I suspect that if I were to tell modern children about what they were missing, they'd probably think, "Ol' Gramps is babbling again."

Chapter 51

A New Season

It's the beginning of summer. Yesterday, with the company of Kiri, my black Lab, I went to the Big Hole River in search of the salmonfly hatch, and some trout feeding on the bounty of this annual emergence of cheeseburgers on the wing.

As it happened, on this stretch of the river that annual emergence of these giant stoneflies hadn't happened, though I managed to catch a couple fish on an imitation stonefly nymph.

This was my first trip to my favorite trout stream since the end of March. We'd had a huge snowpack in the mountains and the river was running at flood stage most of the last two months. The river was still on the high side, but at least it was possible to fish the edges of the water, while watching a parade of drift boats and rubber rafts, mostly with fishing guides at the oars.

It was good to be back home.

After a fun day, I reflected on the last month. Back in the beginning of May I went turkey hunting, the first time in several years. Over the last 30 years or so, I'd hunted turkeys off and on, and never had anything to show for it. The last few years I hadn't hunted them because I needed to draw a permit for our corner of Montana, and every year I struck out. This year, our region changed to "over the counter" for spring turkeys, so I couldn't blame the state for not drawing my name. Even so, the season was already several weeks old before I had the combination of a nice day and no other commitments.

I went to a walk-in hunting area a half-hour's drive away from home. The spot I planned to hunt is just above a small river bottom, full of brush and trees. Above the bottoms, on a little bench, is a strip of grass, a barbed wire fence, and then an alfalfa field. A rutted road runs along the top of the alfalfa field. Driving in I spotted several turkeys in the alfalfa.

After donning camouflage, and packing my hen decoy, call, and, of course, a shotgun, I walked into the area, finding a spot on the grassy strip where I could set up my decoy, try to hide, and do some calling.

It was one of those mornings when spring just jumps right out at you. Contrary to what some people believe, it isn't necessarily quiet in nature. The river was running bank-full with spring runoff, creating its sounds. The river bottom jungle was full of birds, calling out their songs. Ducks were quacking and geese were honking. The rusty gate sound of rooster pheasants announcing their availability for love and romance intruded through the songs. It was just plain noisy.

A coyote crossed the grass and went into the alfalfa, probably in search of voles, or other protein. A rooster pheasant walked across, as well.

A turkey came out of nowhere and flew up into the top of a cottonwood tree a hundred yards away. I worked my call, hoping to entice the bird to come down and see me.

A pair of sandhill cranes flew into the alfalfa, and proceeded to entertain me with their sandhill crane ballet, frequently calling to each other.

The highlight of the morning was seeing a cow moose emerge from the river bottom, casually stepping over the barbed wire fence to feed in the alfalfa. A minute later, a bull moose, its antlers just beginning to poke out the side of his head, joined the cow. Several minutes later a yearling calf moose joined the adults

The moose fed in the alfalfa, working their way toward my spot, as I occasionally took a photo of them.

The flash of the camera evidently gave me away. The cow gave me an "evil eye" look, and decided to leave, going back down to the bottoms. The bull and calf both joined the cow and a minute later I could hear them splashing and swimming their way across the river.

By late morning, no turkeys had blundered in my direction so I decided to go home. As I drove out, across the top of the alfalfa field, I looked across the field and started laughing. A turkey was walking around within mere yards of where I'd set up my stand—and abandoned half an hour earlier.

Patience, I concluded, must be a virtue in this game.

A couple weeks later I had another free day with nice weather and returned to turkey country.

It's almost anticlimactic, but after a couple hours of calling and getting no response I lay back in the grass, covered my eyes with my cap, and took a nap. My slumber was disturbed by a new sound. I cautiously looked out and saw a turkey acting amorously at my decoy. I sat up, raised my gun and shot.

My spring turkey season came to a sudden and unexpectedly successful conclusion.

A week later, my wife and I hit the road for a trip east, for the annual conference of the Outdoor Writers Association of America, which this year would be in Fort Wayne, Indiana.

Our first stop was Minot, North Dakota, where we stayed a couple days with our son, Kevin, and family. As we have done together for over 50 years, we went fishing. The fishing wasn't that productive, though on our first outing I caught a nice smallmouth bass on my fly-rod. Kevin caught a walleye. Both fish came home with us and ended up on the grill along with steak, for a surf and turf dinner.

A few days later we were in northeast Indiana on a preconference junket to Indiana's lake country, as the guests of the Kosciusko County Convention & Visitors Bureau, who were eager to have some outdoor writers from afar take a look at their beautiful area.

After a night in a lakeside resort, with two other writers, Bob from Michigan and Jay from Colorado, I joined a local fishing guide for a morning of guided muskie fishing.

The muskellunge, or muskie, is a first cousin to the northern pike, a fish I've been catching for many years. Still, I'd never done any muskie fishing. The muskie is sometimes called "the fish of 10,000 casts," because of their habit of frustrating anglers. Muskies aren't native to Indiana, but were introduced in the 1970s and thrive in several area lakes.

Our guide, Chae Dolson, grew up fishing the area lakes and occasionally ventured into the bass tournament circuit. Then he discovered muskies. "I like big fish," he commented, and bass held little appeal after that. He lives, eats and breathes muskies from ice-out in the spring until winter freeze-up.

Chae revved up the outboard and we went out into the lake and the three of us non-Hoosiers started throwing out the first of our 10,000 casts. Mainly, we learned that muskies are temperamental. We spotted muskies following our big lures. We'd work the lures in a figure-8 pattern near the boat, trying to entice a strike. Bob had one take his lure, but it was on just a few seconds before it escaped. The typical sightings were of a fish emerging from the dark depths and then slowly disappearing from sight.

The morning was just about done. My shoulders ached from casting heavy lures with heavy rods. I was ready to take a break, though aside from occasional pauses I kept casting. I don't know if the three

of us had gotten in our 10,000 casts, but much to my surprise, a muskie latched onto my lure about ten feet from the boat and a few minutes later Chae had it in the net and in the boat. The muskie wasn't a trophy by any means, because muskies can get seriously big. It measured out at 32 inches long, so still a nice fish. Bob and Jay complimented me on my fishing prowess, though I wasn't doing anything they weren't doing.

It was just pure dumb luck. But, sometimes, pure dumb luck is the key to success.

The next week, our conference over, we spent a little time with our Hoosier friends, Charley and Elizabeth. Charley and I had fished the hex hatch on the Au Sable River in Michigan, the Big Hole in Montana, plus a once in a lifetime trip to northern Saskatchewan for monster pike on a fly rod. He wanted to show me a couple of his local haunts, including a small pond less than a mile from his house. He keeps a small jon boat stashed on the shoreline and we spent the morning slowly paddling around the pond.

I caught several sunfish, or bluegills, if you prefer, on my fly rod. Charley was using an ultra-light spinning rod, catching several bluegills and a small largemouth bass. I hooked one bass but it flipped off the hook before I landed it. Fly-fishing for bluegills might not be as exciting as latching onto a muskie, though many people have suggested that if a bluegill got as big as a muskie, we'd consider that landing one was a major achievement. In any case, a morning spent fishing with a good friend in a quiet Midwest pond is a morning well spent.

A few days later we were back in North Dakota and Kevin and I had one day to go fishing, again. It was a breezy morning but Kevin launched the boat and headed across the lake. We had a fun morning. The wind and waves put the northern pike on the feed and we caught around ten before we figured we'd better quit, as out on the open water, there were lots of whitecaps.

It turned out that there were more than just whitecaps. This was a morning for surfing, with three and four-foot waves that threatened to swamp Kevin's boat. We got drenched with water that came in sheets over the bow. It was a relief to make it back to the boat ramp.

We'd had fun fishing for pike that morning, but boating turned out to be a serious adventure.

This last month had been fun. I don't worry about bucket lists, though if I had one, getting a spring turkey and catching a muskie would be among items I'd check off.

I'd gotten in several days of fishing, along with a bit of adventure, with Kevin, a renewal of things we've been doing together since he was a toddler.

On our trip we had fun visits with dear friends and family, as well as caught fish; all things that make life good.

A few days after getting home we got word that our friend Chuck, a fellow outdoor writer and a fly-fishing guide, as well, died from a sudden heart attack. It happened while at the oars of his drift boat, guiding anglers down the Big Hole River. (Chuck is mentioned in my chapter on rattlesnakes)

All of us who knew him were shocked. We had a tough time accepting that this big, burly man, who spent his summers on the river, and then the fall and winter following his German wirehair pointers in search of sage grouse and pheasants in Montana, and quail in Arizona, and finding time to write about it, would go so suddenly, though some might suggest that for such an outdoorsman, it was a good way to go.

It generally is not given that we will know the time and manner of our deaths. We're not in control of such things. I have concluded, however, that when the Good Lord (not the Grim Reaper) says, "Y'all come," we get up and go.

Before that, I plan to continue living as well and as actively as I have in past years, and as for that old age crisis, I say, "What old age crisis?"

About the Author

Paul Vang grew up around dogs and pheasants on a farm in southern Minnesota. After graduating from St. Olaf College in Northfield, Minnesota, he had a 33 –year career as a manager with the Social Security Administration. After leaving government service he launched a second career as a freelance writer and columnist.

In addition to weekly newspaper columns, his work has been published in many magazines, including *Montana Outdoors, North Dakota Outdoors, Kiwanis, Wheelin' Sportsmen, Blue Ridge,* and *Distinctly Montana.* He has won awards from the Outdoor Writers Association of America and Montana Newspaper Association.

Paul is a past Board member of the Outdoor Writers Association of America and a past president of the Northwest Outdoor Writers Association.

Paul and his wife, Kay, and black Lab, Kiri, live in Butte, Montana, close to good hunting and fly-fishing.

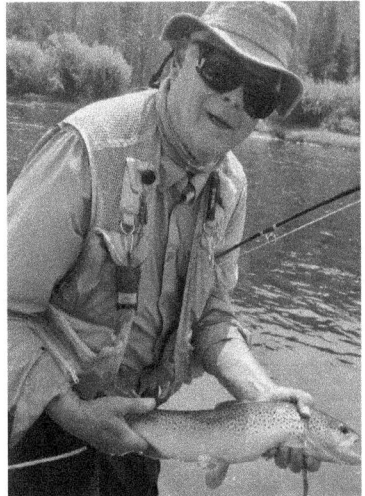

Illustrator

Illustrations are by the author's son, Kevin Vang. In his day job, he's a professor of mathematics at Minot State University, Minot, North Dakota.

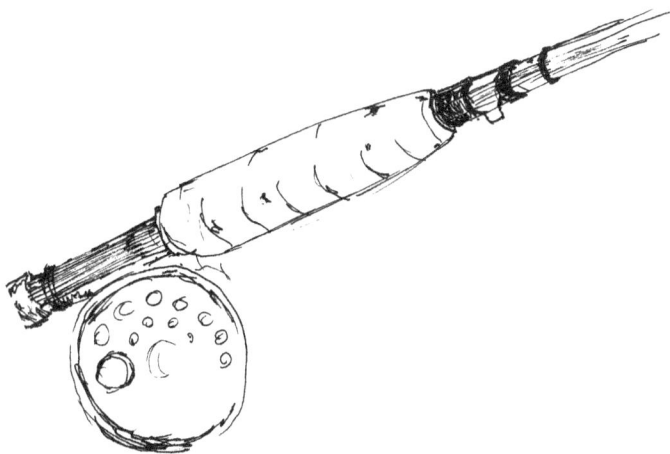

www.ingramcontent.com/pod-product-compliance
Lightning Source LLC
Chambersburg PA
CBHW031502270326
41930CB00006B/202